COGNITIVE THERAPY FOR PERSONALITY DISORDERS:
A SCHEMA-FOCUSED APPROACH

Revised Edition

Jeffrey E. Young, PhD

Director
Cognitive Therapy Centers of New York
and Fairfield County
(Connecticut)

Department of Psychiatry
Columbia University

Professional Resource Press
Sarasota, Florida

Published by
Professional Resource Press
(An imprint of the Professional Resource Exchange, Inc.)
Post Office Box 15560
Sarasota, FL 34277-1560

Printed in the United States of America

The copy editor for this book was Patricia Hammond, the managing editor was Debbie Fink, the production coordinator was Laurie Girsch, and the cover designer was Bill Tabler.

Library of Congress Cataloging-in-Publication Data

Young, Jeffrey E. date.
    Cognitive therapy for personality disorders : a schema-focused approach / Jeffrey E. Young. -- Rev. ed.
        p.   cm. -- (Practitioner's resource series)
    Includes bibliographical references and index.
    ISBN 1-56887-006-X
    1. Personality disorders--Treatment. 2. Schema-focused cognitive therapy. I. Title. II. Series.
    [DNLM: 1. Personality Disorders--therapy. 2. Cognitive Therapy--methods. WM 190 Y73c 1994]
RC554.Y68   1994
616.85'8--dc20
DNLM/DLC
for Library of Congress   94-13880
                                                                   CIP

ACKNOWLEDGEMENTS

The author would like to express appreciation to the following people: Wayne Swift, Janet Klosko, Dan and Tara Goleman, Richard Sackett, William Zangwill, Arthur Weinberger, and Center colleagues for their invaluable feedback and support in the development of this approach; Tim Beck, for his important role in guiding the author's professional growth; and to his family for their ongoing confidence in him - his father, mother, Stephen, Debbie, and Hannes.

SERIES PREFACE

As a publisher of books, cassettes, and continuing education programs, the Professional Resource Press and Professional Resource Exchange, Inc. strive to provide mental health professionals with highly applied resources that can be used to enhance clinical skills and expand practical knowledge.

All the titles in the *Practitioner's Resource Series* are designed to provide important new information on topics of vital concern to psychologists, clinical social workers, marriage and family therapists, psychiatrists, and other mental health professionals.

Although the focus and content of each book in this series will be quite different, there will be notable similarities:

1. Each title in the series will address a timely topic of critical clinical importance.
2. The target audience for each title will be practicing mental health professionals. Our authors were chosen for their ability to provide concrete "how-to-do-it" guidance to colleagues who are trying to increase their competence in dealing with complex clinical problems.
3. The information provided in these books will represent "state-of-the-art" information and techniques derived from both clinical experience and empirical research. Each of these guide books will include references and resources for those who wish to pursue more advanced study of the discussed topics.

4. The authors will provide numerous case studies, specific recommendations for practice, and the types of "nitty-gritty" details that clinicians need before they can incorporate new concepts and procedures into their practices.

We feel that one of the unique assets of the Professional Resource Press is that all of its editorial decisions are made by mental health professionals. The publisher, all editorial consultants, and all reviewers are practicing psychologists, marriage and family therapists, clinical social workers, and psychiatrists.

If there are other topics you would like to see addressed in this series, please let me know.

Lawrence G. Ritt, Publisher

ABSTRACT

Personality disorders are among the most resistant clinical problems presented to therapists - and they are evident in the majority of private practice patients. This book discusses schema-focused therapy, an integrative approach developed by the author to treat characterological patients including borderline, narcissistic, avoidant, dependent, obsessive-compulsive, passive-aggressive, and histrionic personality disorders. Schema-focused treatment techniques have also been utilized in preventing relapse with depression, anxiety disorders, and substance abuse and in the treatment of physical and psychological abuse, eating disorders, and chronic pain. Dr. Young's model is a pioneering integration of cognitive behavior therapy with gestalt, object relations, and psychoanalytic approaches. It expands on conventional cognitive behavior therapy by placing more emphasis on the therapeutic relationship, affective experience, and the discussion of early life experiences. In addition to presenting the rationale, theory, and practical techniques of schema-focused therapy, this book includes an extended case example, and revised editions of the Schema Questionnaire, Client's Guide, and schema listings.

TABLE OF CONTENTS

APPLICATION OF SCHEMA-
FOCUSED COGNITIVE THERAPY *(Continued)*

APPENDICES *(Continued)*

COGNITIVE THERAPY
FOR PERSONALITY DISORDERS:
A SCHEMA-FOCUSED APPROACH

RATIONALE*

INTRODUCTION

One of the new challenges for cognitive therapy today is to develop effective treatment strategies for working with patients with personality disorders and other diffi- cult, chronic patients.

The first section will outline seven characteristics that patients must have in order to succeed in short-term cognitive therapy. "Short-term cognitive therapy" refers to the 16- to 20-session cognitive therapy approach origi- nally developed by Beck and his colleagues (1979) for de- pression. The section will go on to demonstrate how patients with personality disorders and other difficult pa- tients violate some of these basic assumptions.

The next section will discuss how short-term cognitive therapy can be adapted and expanded to describe more fully what we observe in patients with personality disor- ders. A clinical theory of schemas will be outlined brief- ly. The final sections will describe the adaptation of short-term cognitive therapy techniques to overcome the obstacles presented by patients with personality disorders. This new approach is called "Schema-Focused Cognitive Therapy."

---

*Names and identifying characteristics of persons in all case examples have been disguised thoroughly to protect privacy.

ASSUMPTIONS IN SHORT-TERM COGNITIVE THERAPY

Short-term cognitive therapy makes seven assumptions about patients:

1. *Patients have access to feelings with brief training.* In short-term cognitive therapy we assume that with a relatively short amount of training we can teach patients to report when they are feeling anxious, sad, angry, guilty, or another emotion. However, in a variety of patients with longer-term disorders, this ability to report their feelings does not seem to be present. Many patients are blocked and out of touch with what they feel; for these patients we have to modify the short-term cognitive therapy approach.

2. The second assumption in short-term cognitive therapy is that *the patient has access to thoughts and images with brief training.* Many patients with personality disorders cannot report to us what their automatic thoughts are; or, they claim not to have images. For these patients as well, we have to develop new strategies that are not currently available in short-term cognitive therapy.

3. Short-term cognitive therapy presumes that *the patient has identifiable problems on which to focus.* Some difficult patients have vague or hard-to-define problems. They may have a general malaise for which they are not able to identify specific triggers. We have to modify short-term cognitive therapy to work with patients for whom there are no specific target problems.

4. Short-term cognitive therapy assumes that *the patient has motivation to do homework assignments and to learn self-control strategies.* However, in working with many longer-term patients, we find that they are unwilling or unable to do homework assignments and show tremendous resistance to learning self-control strategies. These patients seem far more motivated to lean on the therapist and to obtain support than to learn strategies for helping themselves.

5. Short-term cognitive therapy assumes that *the patient can engage in a collaborative relationship with the therapist within a few sessions.* However, with

many patients, engaging them in a collaborative relationship is nearly impossible. The therapist/patient relationship is so problematic that some patients either become consumed in trying to get the therapist to meet their needs or are so disengaged and hostile that they are unable to collaborate.

6. The sixth assumption is that *difficulties in the therapeutic relationship are not a major problem focus.* However, in many patients with personality disorders, if we assume that the problems in the therapeutic relationship are merely obstacles to overcome so that we can then get on with short-term cognitive therapy, we often miss the real core of the problem. In many patients with personality disorders, the core of their problem is interpersonal, and one of the best arenas for observing these problems is in the therapeutic relationship. With these patients, dealing with the therapeutic relationship as a primary focus of therapy becomes far more important; unfortunately, short-term cognitive therapy has little to say about how to work in depth with the therapeutic relationship.

7. A seventh assumption in short-term cognitive therapy is that *all cognitions and behavior patterns can be changed through empirical analysis, logical discourse, experimentation, gradual steps, and practice.* With many chronic patients, their cognitions and self-defeating behavior patterns are extremely resistant to modification solely through short-term cognitive behavioral techniques. Such patients may repeatedly report that they understand intellectually what the therapist is demonstrating, but that emotionally their feelings, behaviors, and beliefs remain unchanged. Even after months of chipping away at such beliefs and behavior patterns, there is often no change or improvement. Such patients are often hopeless about modifying their core beliefs or behavior patterns, insisting that these cognitions and behaviors are too much a part of themselves to change at this point in their lives.

The five patients described below illustrate how these assumptions can be violated. Sally was a 20-year-old student who spent the first 10 sessions sitting in the corner, facing away from the therapist. She would give only terse "yes" or "no" answers to questions. When the therapist asked what she wanted to work on or what she felt, she said she did not know. Sally presented a variety of problems for short-term cognitive therapy. First, her sitting in the corner made it very difficult to collaborate. Second, her inability to state a problem or to describe her feelings made it difficult to find a problem focus or to elicit emotions and their associated automatic thoughts.

Sam was a 45-year-old attorney who claimed he did not feel or think about anything. He claimed to be numb all the time, with several anxiety symptoms, but reported no thoughts before or during his periods of anxiety and numbness. He appeared very controlled and highly intelligent. With this patient we also found a major difficulty in undertaking short-term cognitive therapy. The patient reported no automatic thoughts connected with his anxiety symptoms, and furthermore there seemed to be no specific trigger events that set off his symptoms.

Karl was a 40-year-old writer who avoided most social contact because he was afraid he would sound foolish to other people. He would not do homework assignments designed to increase social contact, no matter how minimal the contact was. Karl presented a problem because he was unable or unwilling to do homework assignments, yet the crux of the problem was his avoidance of social contact. Even though he was able to report his thoughts and feelings, because he was unwilling to take even minimal steps to initiate social contact, short-term cognitive therapy seemed to be perpetually at an impasse with him.

Kathleen was a 21-year-old college student who lived at home and felt chronically depressed. She would not do cognitive homework assignments because she wanted the therapist to make her better by being available as often as possible, day and night. Every time the therapist suggested homework assignments, Kathleen refused to do them. She interpreted these assignments as an unwillingness on the part of the therapist to be there for her when she needed him.

Mark was a 43-year-old man who entered therapy frustrated because he could not find a suitable woman to marry. Upon closer examination, Mark's pattern in relationships was to bail out soon after women expressed strong affection and love toward him. He would remain indefinitely with women who were either ambivalent or rejecting toward him. When he got close to women who loved him, he would devalue them by asking why anyone worthwhile would want to get close to him. His feelings of unlovability proved completely resistant to the therapist's attempts at collaborative empiricism of any sort. The rigidity of his cognitions and behaviors made short-term cognitive therapy frustrating and unrewarding. Mark was unable to defend these beliefs, except by saying he "just felt defective." Yet his cognitions, emotions, and behaviors remained dysfunctional.

Each of these five patients illustrates one or more of the ways in which short-term cognitive therapy does not fit with certain patients. The next section will attempt to explain why such patients are often diagnosed with personality disorders, and why chronic, difficult patients frequently fail to respond to short-term cognitive therapy.

PERSONALITY DISORDERS
AND COGNITIVE THERAPY

Rigidity. Short-term cognitive therapy assumes a certain flexibility on the part of patients, an assumption that does not hold true in most personality disorders. Typically, the cognitive therapist employs a variety of strategies to help patients see the inaccuracy or maladaptiveness of their thinking. The therapist assumes that, with enough practice and rehearsal, cognitions and behavior patterns are flexible enough to be modified through collaborative empiricism.

However, according to *DSM-IV* (American Psychiatric Association, 1994), and consistent with our own clinical experience, one of the hallmarks of personality disorders is the presence of pervasive, inflexible patterns that are enduring (*DSM-IV*, p. 629). Millon (1981) reinforces this point by specifying *adaptive inflexibility* and *vicious circles* as two of the major criteria for personality pathology: "the alternative strategies the individual employs for relating to others, for achieving goals, and for coping with stress are not only few in number but appear to be practiced rigidly" (p. 9).

He elaborates on this process through which patients with personality disorders set up vicious cycles of self-defeating sequences:

Maneuvers such as protective constriction, cognitive distortion, and behavior generalization are processes by which individuals restrict their opportunities for new learning, misconstrue essentially benign events, and

5

provoke reactions from others that reactivate earlier problems. (Millon, 1981, p. 9)

He goes on to contrast personality disorders with "symptom disorders" such as depression:

Personality patterns are deeply embedded and pervasive, and are likely to persist, essentially unmodified, over long periods of time . . . Symptom disorders possess well-delineated clinical features that are less difficult to modify than the ingrained personal traits from which they arise. (Millon, 1981, p. 10)

Finally, Millon points out that personality traits "feel right" to the individual who possesses them ("ego syntonic").

Avoidance.   Short-term cognitive therapy assumes that patients have relatively free access to their thoughts and feelings. In many personality disorders, however, thoughts and feelings are often avoided, or blocked out, because they are painful. This "cognitive avoidance" or "affective avoidance" can be explained as the result of aversive conditioning: anxiety and depression have become conditioned to memories and associations, leading to avoidance. This becomes a chronic strategy that can then defeat short-term cognitive treatment.

The traditional psychoanalytic view is that defenses such as repression (i.e., avoidance) are most effective in personality disorders:

The defenses of patients with personality disorders have been part of the warp and woof of their life histories and of their personal identities. However maladaptive their defenses may be, they represent homeostatic solutions to inner problems. . . . Breaching their defenses evokes enormous anxiety and depression. (Kaplan & Sadock, 1985, p. 965)

Millon (1981) states that: "Repression thwarts the individual from 'unlearning' disturbed feelings or learning new, potentially more constructive ways of coping with them" (p. 101).

Although cognitive therapists reject much of psychoanalytic theory, it is undeniable that many difficult, chronic patients seem actively to avoid looking at their deepest cognitions and emotions. Regardless of how this phenomenon is explained, therapists still must develop therapeutic strategies to deal with this avoidance, or else they will be continually stymied by personality disorders.

Interpersonal Difficulties. The third hallmark of patients with personality disorders is their dysfunctional interpersonal relationships. In fact, most of the *DSM-IV* personality disorder definitions highlight these interpersonal difficulties, including: histrionic, schizoid, dependent, paranoid, and borderline disorders.

To summarize, three characteristics of personality disorders - rigidity, avoidance, and long-term interpersonal difficulties - lead to considerable difficulty in applying short-term cognitive therapy, as illustrated by the case examples earlier. The next section describes an expanded clinical theory that takes these three factors into account.

SCHEMA THEORY

To permit the more complete conceptualization and treatment of patients with personality disorders, the following four theoretical constructs are proposed as an expansion of the short-term cognitive model proposed by Beck and his colleagues (1979):

1. Early Maladaptive Schemas
2. Schema Maintenance
3. Schema Avoidance
4. Schema Compensation

This expansion of terms (to be elaborated upon later) is not intended as a comprehensive theory of psychopathology or personality, but rather as a "convenient clinical heuristic" (Segal, 1988). We offer a straightforward working theory, comprehensible to patients, that enables patients and therapists to communicate about deeper-level phonomena that have not yet been incorporated into most short-term cognitive behavior therapies. The constructs proposed here have not yet been tested empirically, and so must be viewed as speculative. Furthermore, although we often speak to patients about schemas as if they exist structurally and have a life and force of their own, we do this only for ease of communication, aware that this is an unsophisticated explanation of a hypothetical construct.

In some of his earliest work, Beck (1967) emphasized the importance of schemas in depression:

> A schema is a [cognitive] structure for screening, coding, and evaluating the stimuli that impinge on the organism . . . On the basis of the matrix of schemas, the individual is able to orient himself in relation to time and space and to categorize and interpret experiences in a meaningful way. (p. 283)

Beck goes on to make a number of additional points about schemas. He hypothesizes that schemas may account for the repetitive themes in free associations, images, and dreams. He notes that they may be inactive at one point in time, and then "energized or de-energized rapidly as a result of changes in the type of input from the environment" (1967, p. 284).

Another important observation Beck makes is that schemas bias our interpretations of events in a consistent manner. These biases in "psychopathology" are "reflected in the typical misconceptions, distorted attitudes, invalid premises, and unrealistic goals and expectations" (1967, p. 284).

Segal (1988) provides the following definition of schemas, drawn from a consensus of many researchers: "Organized elements of past reactions and experience that form a relatively cohesive and persistent body of knowledge capable of guiding subsequent perception and appraisals" (p. 147). Our own concept of "schema" is consistent with this definition and with Beck's, but is more limited and specific, as outlined later.

Segal goes on to contrast several different models of schemas. These models offer differing explanations regarding: (a) the relationship between moods and personal constructs, and (b) the interconnectedness of personal constructs within the self-system.

We will not attempt to provide a competing theory of schemas, nor will we ally with any of the specific existing approaches. Instead, the main purpose of the schema theory presented below is to provide direction for the clinical interventions outlined later. Only enough theory is included to guide the therapist in developing practical case conceptualizations that can be explained to patients in simple terms, and that will lead to effective intervention strategies.

EARLY MALADAPTIVE SCHEMAS

Short-term cognitive therapy focuses primarily on three levels of cognitive phenomena: automatic thoughts, cognitive distortions, and underlying assumptions. We are proposing a primary emphasis on the deepest level of cognition, the Early Maladaptive Schema (EMS). Although Beck and his associates (1979, p. 304) refer to the importance of schemas in treatment, they have offered very few specific treatment guidelines in their treatment protocols to date.

Early Maladaptive Schemas refer to extremely stable and enduring themes that develop during childhood and are elaborated upon throughout an individual's lifetime. These schemas serve as templates for the processing of later experience. Structurally, this concept of schema is similar to Lakatos' "metaphysical hard-core":

[A] deep, relatively indisputable metaphysical hardcore . . . identified essentially in the tacit self-knowledge that has been progressively elaborated during the course of development and that . . . is for individuals a kind of implicit general view of themselves. (Cited in Guidano & Liotti, 1983, p. 66)

Early Maladaptive Schemas have several defining characteristics:

1. Most Early Maladaptive Schemas are unconditional beliefs about oneself in relation to the environment. Schemas are *a priori* truths that are implicit and taken for granted. Guidano and Liotti state that: "The deep structure's irrefutability is therefore a real . . . necessity. For us as individuals, our own tacit self-knowledge is a constitutive part of ourselves; with no real alternatives" (1983, p. 67).

   We can contrast EMS's with underlying assumptions. Underlying assumptions hold out the possibility of success for an individual. "If I can be perfect, if I can please other people all the time, if I am loved, then I am worthwhile." Sche-

9

mas in contrast are usually unconditional, and therefore more rigid. "No matter what I do: I'm incompetent, unlovable, ugly; I'll be abandoned; I'll be punished." When the schema is activated, individuals believe that they can, at best, delay or hide the inevitable bad outcome such as rejection or punishment.

2. Early Maladaptive Schemas are self-perpetuating, and therefore much more resistant to change. Because schemas are developed early in life, they often form the core of an individual's self-concept and conception of the environment. These schemas are comfortable and familiar, and when challenged, the individual will distort information to maintain the validity of the schema. The threat of schematic change is too disruptive to the core cognitive organization. Therefore the individual automatically engages in a variety of cognitive maneuvers (described later) to maintain the schema intact.

Millon (1981) makes the same point in his discussion of personality disorders:

> Once individuals acquire a system of expectancies, they respond with increasing alertness to similar elements in their life situation . . . The importance of expectancies, sensitivities, and language habits lies in the fact that they lead to the distortion of objective realities. (p. 102)

Guidano and Liotti (1983) similarly emphasize the circular nature of schemas:

> The selection of data from outside reality that are coherent with self-image obviously confirms--in an automatic and circular way--the perceived personal iden tity . . . .
> Let us consider a young woman wh. has developed a self-image as "intrinsically unlovable" . . . Since every time she is abandoned she processes the data derived from the experience on the basis of her self-image (so that it is reconfirmed and made more stable each time), little by little her

own "unlovableness" becomes something certain and "proved." (pp. 88-89)

3. Early Maladaptive Schemas, by definition, must be dysfunctional in some significant and recurring manner. We hypothesize that they can lead directly or indirectly to psychological distress like depression or panic; to loneliness or to destructive relationships; to inadequate work performance; to addictions like alcohol, drugs, or overeating; or to psychosomatic disorders like ulcers or insomnia.

4. Early Maladaptive Schemas are usually activated by events in the environment relevant to the particular schema. For example, when an adult with an incompetence/failure schema is assigned a difficult task in which performance will be scrutinized, the schema erupts. Thoughts begin to arise such as: "I can't handle this. I'll fail. I'll make a fool of myself." These thoughts are usually accompanied by a high level of affective arousal, in this case anxiety. Depending on the circumstances and the particular schema, the individual might experience other emotions, such as sadness, shame, guilt, or anger.

5. EMS's are usually much more closely tied to high levels of affect when activated than are underlying assumptions. For example, when some patients discover that they hold the assumption that they must be approved of by everyone, it is rare for them to break down in tears or begin shaking with anxiety. However, when patients identify an Early Maladaptive Schema, such as defectiveness/unlovability, there is often a high level of affective arousal.

6. Finally, Early Maladaptive Schemas seem to be the result of dysfunctional experiences with parents, siblings, and peers during the first few years of an individual's life. Rather than resulting from isolated traumatic events, most schemas are probably caused by ongoing patterns of everyday noxious experiences with family members and peers which cumulatively strengthen the schema. For example, a child who is repeatedly criticized when performance does not meet parental standards is prone to develop the incompetence/failure schema.

11

Millon (1981) emphasizes the persisting influences of early negative experience:

> Significant experiences of early life may never recur again, but their effects remain and leave their mark . . . they are registered as memories, a permanent trace and an embedded internal stimulus . . . Once registered, the effects of the past are indelible, incessant and inescapable . . . .
>
> The residuals of the past do more than passively contribute their share to the present . . . they guide, shape or distort the character of current events. Not only are they ever present, then, but they operate insidiously to transform new stimulus experiences in line with past. (p. 101)

Fifteen Early Maladaptive Schemas have been identified thus far.* These 15 encompass almost all of the longer-term patients in our clinical practices. Most chronic psychotherapy patients have more than one of these core schemas. Furthermore, each schema can have many variations on the same theme. Table 1 (pp. 13-14) lists the 15 EMS's, along with definitions of each schema. The schemas are grouped into four broad categories, corresponding to four general areas of functioning: (a) Autonomy, (b) Connectedness, (c) Worthiness, and (d) Expectations and Limits. (For a more complete discussion of these categories, along with a preliminary discussion of possible developmental antecedents to schemas see Appendix A, pp. 53-56.)

SCHEMA MAINTENANCE

We have also identified three major schema processes: schema maintenance, schema avoidance, and schema compensation. These processes explain how schemas function within the individual. They explain how schemas are maintained and how they are avoided, and how patients sometimes adapt to schemas by overcompensation. These processes can occur within the cognitive realm, the affective domain, and in long-term behavioral functioning.

---

*The main text and tables refer to the 15 Early Maladaptive Schemas and four schema domains identified in 1990. For the most recent revision of schemas and domains, see Appendix B (pp. 57-62). Appendices C and D (pp. 63-90) are based on intermediate versions of the schemas, and thus differ from both the text and Appendix B.

TABLE 1: EARLY MALADAPTIVE SCHEMAS WITH DEFINITIONS AND DOMAINS

DOMAIN	SCHEMAS WITH DEFINITIONS
I. AUTONOMY	1. DEPENDENCE Belief that one is unable to function on one's own.
	2. SUBJUGATION/LACK OF INDIVIDUATION The voluntary or involuntary sacrifice of one's own needs to satisfy others' needs, often with an accompanying failure to recognize one's own needs.
	3. VULNERABILITY TO HARM AND ILLNESS The fear that disaster is about to strike at any time (natural, criminal, medical, or financial).
	4. FEAR OF LOSING SELF-CONTROL The fear that one will involuntarily lose control of one's own behavior, impulses, emotions, mind, body, and so on.
II. CONNECTEDNESS	5. EMOTIONAL DEPRIVATION The expectation that one's needs for nurturance, empathy, affection, and caring will never be adequately met by others.
	6. ABANDONMENT/LOSS Fear that one will imminently lose significant others and then be emotionally isolated forever.
	7. MISTRUST The expectation that others will willfully hurt, abuse, cheat, lie, manipulate, or take advantage.
	8. SOCIAL ISOLATION/ALIENATION The feeling that one is isolated from the rest of the world, different from other people, and/or not a part of any group or community.
III. WORTHINESS	9. DEFECTIVENESS/UNLOVABILITY The feeling that one is inwardly defective and flawed; or that one would be fundamentally unlovable to significant others if exposed.

TABLE 1 (Continued)

DOMAIN	SCHEMAS WITH DEFINITIONS
	10. SOCIAL UNDESIRABILITY The belief that one is <u>outwardly</u> undesirable to others (e.g., ugly, sexually undesirable, low in status, poor in conversational skills, dull).
	11. INCOMPETENCE/FAILURE The belief that one cannot perform competently in areas of achievement (school, career), daily responsibilities to oneself or others, or decision making.
	12. GUILT/PUNISHMENT The belief that one is morally or ethically bad or irresponsible, and deserving of harsh criticism or punishment.
	13. SHAME/EMBARRASSMENT Recurrent feelings of shame or self-consciousness, experienced because one believes that one's inadequacies (as reflected in any of the other schemas) are totally unacceptable to others and are exposed.
IV. EXPECTATIONS AND LIMITS	14. UNRELENTING STANDARDS The relentless striving to meet extremely high expectations of oneself, at the expense of happiness, pleasure, health, sense of accomplishment, or satisfying relationships.
	15. ENTITLEMENT/INSUFFICIENT LIMITS Insistence that one should be able to do, say, or have whatever one wants immediately. Disregard for: what others consider reasonable, what is actually feasible, the time or patience usually required, or the costs to others. May include difficulty with self-discipline.

14

We emphasized earlier that, for many patients, Early Maladaptive Schemas form the cornerstone of their self-concepts. EMS's are central to the organization of personality. *Schema maintenance* refers to processes by which these Early Maladaptive Schemas are reinforced. These processes include both cognitive distortions and self-defeating behavior patterns. Schema maintenance processes account for the rigidity which is so characteristic of personality disorders.

At the cognitive level, schema maintenance is usually accomplished by highlighting or exaggerating information that confirms the schema, and by negating, minimizing, or denying information that contradicts the schema. Many of these schema maintenance processes have already been described by Beck as cognitive distortions (Beck, 1967). Some of the most common distortions are magnification, minimization, selective abstraction, and overgeneralization. When therapists begin to doubt or challenge these schemas, they often encounter enormous resistance. The patient often actively attempts to prove to the therapist that the schema is true. Information is distorted to maintain schemas intact.

At the behavioral level, schema maintenance is achieved through self-defeating behavior patterns. These *schema-driven behavior patterns* may have been adaptive and functional in the patient's early family environment. In later life, outside the original family setting, these behaviors often are self-defeating and ultimately serve to reinforce patients' schemas.

For example, a woman with the subjugation schema may repeatedly select men who are domineering. By doing so, she adopts a subordinate role which feels comfortable and familiar, while reinforcing her view of herself as subjugated. Maladaptive partner selection is one of the most common mechanisms through which schemas are maintained.

Schema maintenance often leads patients to feel *hopeless* about changing their schemas, even after they learn to recognize and monitor them. Early Maladaptive Schemas seem so inextricably tied to their view of themselves that many patients cannot conceive of changing them, no matter how motivated they are.

To summarize, cognitive filters and self-defeating behaviors are the primary mechanisms of schema maintenance, and together serve to perpetuate schemas, making them increasingly inflexible.

SCHEMA AVOIDANCE

The importance of avoidance as a characteristic of personality disorders has already been emphasized. To reiterate, when EMS's are triggered, the individual usually experiences a high level of affect, such as intense anger, anxiety, sadness, or guilt. This emotional intensity is usually unpleasant; therefore the individual often develops both volitional and automatic processes for avoiding either the triggering of the schema or the experience of affect connected to the schema. These processes can be explained as aversive conditioning.

We have observed several types of schema avoidance. Some of these processes involve *cognitive avoidance*. Cognitive avoidance refers to automatic or volitional attempts to block thoughts or images that might trigger the schema. For example, when some patients are asked to recall an event that triggers a schema, they reply: "I don't want to think about that" or "I forgot"; and, if asked to visualize the situation, they might close their eyes and say, "All I see is a blank screen."

Some of these cognitive avoidance processes overlap with the psychoanalytic concept of defense mechanisms. Examples of these include repression, suppression, and denial. Another strategy for cognitive avoidance can be depersonalization, a process by which patients remove themselves psychologically from the situation that triggers an EMS. Compulsive behavior can often serve the same function of distracting patients from focusing their thoughts on potentially upsetting life events that trigger schemas.

A second type of schema avoidance process is *affective avoidance*. Affective avoidance refers to automatic or volitional attempts to block feelings that are triggered by schemas. For example, some borderline patients have reported to us that they cut their wrists to numb themselves to the unbearable pain triggered by early schemas. More frequently, though, we observe patients who seem to have learned automatic processes for dulling their emotional experience. Such patients rarely feel extreme anger, sadness, or anxiety, even in situations that would certainly trigger these emotions for most other people. This affective avoidance can take place even when there is no cognitive avoidance. In other words, in the face of a disruptive life event, some patients are fully capable of reporting their cognitions, yet deny experiencing the emotions that would normally accompany these thoughts. The result of this affective avoidance process seems to be that avoidant patients experience more chronic, diffuse, generalized emotions and psychosomatic symptoms, in comparison with nonavoidant patients who experience more intense, acute emotions that pass quickly, followed by periods of normal mood.

The final type of schema avoidance is *behavioral avoidance*. Behavioral avoidance refers to the tendency of many patients to avoid real-life situations or circumstances that might trigger painful schemas. At its most extreme, behavioral avoidance can be demonstrated through social isolation, agoraphobia, or failure to attempt any type of productive career or family responsibilities.

As an example of a less extreme form of behavioral avoidance, consider a male patient with the incompetence/failure schema. He assumes *a priori* that he will fail at any work task. Based on this premise, he avoids committing himself to a demanding career and does not seek promotions or advancement on the job. This under-achievement is an example of a schema-driven process. By not pursuing challenges, he avoids the pain of what he anticipates will be inevitable failure; however, by maintaining the *status quo* at work, he also reinforces his view of himself as incompetent. Thus, schema avoidance behaviors protect individuals from committing themselves fully to situations that might trigger early schemas; yet this process of noncommitment is itself self-defeating and never challenges the validity of the schema itself.

In summary, all three major types of schema avoidance - cognitive, affective, and behavioral - allow patients to escape the pain associated with their EMS's. However, the price of this avoidance is: (a) the schema may never be brought into the open and questioned, and (b) life experiences are precluded that might disprove the validity of these schemas.

SCHEMA COMPENSATION

Schema compensation refers to processes that overcompensate for Early Maladaptive Schemas. We have observed that many patients adopt cognitive or behavioral styles that seem to be the *opposite* of what we would predict from a knowledge of their early schemas. (Analysts discuss the notion of reaction formation, which is a related concept.) For example, some patients who have experienced significant emotional deprivation as children behave in a narcissistic manner as adults. Their apparent sense of entitlement obscures the underlying deprivation.

Schema compensation is often functional, to a certain extent. For example, instead of behaving in a manner that reinforces a sense of deprivation, some patients put all their effort into getting these needs met. Unfortunately, these attempts often overshoot the mark and ultimately backfire. The narcissistic patient may end up alienating friends, spouses, and colleagues, returning once again to a state of deprivation.

The counterdependent patient may reject all help from others and end up excessively self-reliant - unable to ask for help even when necessary and appropriate. Or the patient with an incompetence schema may vehemently deny the validity of any criticism - and thus never receive the benefit of constructive feedback that might lead to greater competence or success.

Schema compensation processes may be viewed as partially successful attempts by patients to challenge their schemas. Unfortunately, schema compensation almost always involves a failure to recognize the underlying vulnerability, and therefore leaves the patient unprepared for the powerful emotional pain if schema compensation fails and the schema erupts. Furthermore, schema-driven behaviors that overcompensate may infringe unfairly on the rights of others, and ultimately lead to deleterious real-life consequences.

Table 2 (p. 19) highlights the distinctions between the three major types of schema-driven behaviors: schema maintenance, compensation, and avoidance behaviors. For each schema, the table provides an example of each process, as well as an example of *adaptive* behavior that is not schema-driven, and is thus typical of individuals who do *not* have the schema in question.

APPLICATION OF SCHEMA-FOCUSED COGNITIVE THERAPY

CONCEPTUALIZING THE CASE

Identifying Schemas. Eight steps are required to identify schemas. These steps, briefly, are:

TABLE 2: ILLUSTRATIVE EXAMPLES OF SCHEMA-DRIVEN BEHAVIORAL PROCESSES

EARLY SCHEMA	SCHEMA MAINTENANCE BEHAVIOR	SCHEMA COMPENSATION BEHAVIOR	SCHEMA AVOIDANCE BEHAVIOR	ADAPTIVE BEHAVIOR
Dependence	Relies totally on others to write paper.	Does the paper without any help, even when appropriate.	Procrastinates the paper.	Does the paper with some help if needed.
Emotional Deprivation	Selects a partner who is unavailable.	Is extremely demanding of a partner.	Avoids intimacy entirely.	Has a close, mutual relationship, with equal give and take.
Subjugation	Pleases other people; doesn't worry about self.	Won't do anything others want.	Procrastinates action.	Finds balance between own needs and others'.
Incompetence/Failure	Does a project half-heartedly; screws it up.	Won't admit errors when pointed out.	Procrastinates or refuses project.	Does project well and accepts valid advice.
Defectiveness/ Unlovability	Selects a very critical partner.	Demands constant admiration and attention.	Avoids close relationships.	Has close relationships where both partners express strength and vulnerabilities.
Social Isolation/ Alienation	Attends group activities but stays on periphery.	Attacks group members for their values.	Avoids groups entirely.	Joins in group activities wholeheartedly.

1. Identify presenting symptoms and problems in the initial evaluation session. Obtain a brief focused life history.
2. Administer the Multimodal Life History Inventory (A. Lazarus & C. Lazarus, 1991) and the Schema Questionnaire (Second Edition) (SQ; see Appendix C, pp. 63-77).
3. Educate the patient about schemas and discuss the SQ.
4. Trigger schemas in the session and outside the session through: imagery, discussing upsetting events in the past and present, examining the therapeutic relationship, recommending relevant books and movies, reviewing dreams, and assigning homework.
5. Confront schema avoidance and schema compensation.
6. Identify schema-driven behaviors: schema maintenance, avoidance, and compensation.
7. Integrate the information above into a coherent conceptualization of the patient. Link presenting problems, childhood experiences (origins), adolescent and adult behavioral patterns, emotions, and the therapeutic relationship with the EMS's. Get feedback from the patient.
8. Distinguish between primary, secondary, and associated schemas. Target a core schema for the change process.

The Evaluation. The first stage in identifying schemas is the evaluation session. During the evaluation session, the therapist tries to identify the presenting symptoms and problems. The therapist begins to form connections among specific emotions, symptoms, life problems, and schemas. During the course of inquiry about life events and symptoms, hypotheses are developed about possible themes. Issues of autonomy, connectedness, worthiness, reasonable expectations, and realistic limits are explored to see if any of these present significant problems for the patient.

In order to illustrate the process of identifying and changing schemas, we will present a patient named Carla, a 22-year-old woman in her first year of law school when she initially came for treatment.

When Carla came for her first session, the symptoms she presented were panic, agitation, depression, lethargy, tiredness, difficulty sleeping, depersonalization, and a sense of being lost. In terms of specific life events, she attributed these feelings to (a) "Pushing myself at school but not knowing why," (b) questioning her own identity ("Who am I?"), (c) not having any close friends or relationships, and (d) difficulties with her family. Her Beck Depression Inventory score was 17, with particularly high scores on items having to do with guilt, being disgusted with herself, and blaming herself all the time for her faults.

Questionnaires. The second stage in the identification process is the administration of the Multimodal Life History Questionnaire and the Schema Questionnaire. These are usually assigned as homework during the weeks between sessions two and four.

On Carla's Life History Questionnaire, she indicated that the major behavior problems she wanted to change were: "I want to have more balance in my life," and "I cannot concentrate on anything any more." She listed as her major fears: fear of failure, fear of being alone, fear of losing people who were important to her, and fear of not being able to share her life with others. She also reported continual feelings of being cold but not knowing what the cold feelings were from, and of depersonalizing periodically.

In the section regarding images, Carla reported having unpleasant childhood images; helpless images and lonely images. She pictured herself as being hurt, not being able to cope, losing control, hurting others, failing, and being trapped. In the section regarding her view of herself, Carla indicated that she saw herself as useless, unlovable, unattractive, undesirable, and not being able to do anything right.

In the section having to do with values and underlying assumptions, Carla indicated very strong belief in the statement, "It is my responsibility to make other people happy." She also endorsed statements that she should be good at everything she does; that it is very important to please other people; and that she should strive for perfection. In the sentence completion section, she completed the stem, "Ever since I was a child . . ." by writing, ". . . I've loved my family more than myself." Carla added an addendum to the questionnaire in which she wrote the following:

> Over the past 4 months I have been troubled by everything and anything. I have been tense, irritable, and depressed most of the time. I do not seem to be

able to relax or get any relief from any activity. I worry constantly. I'm having a hard time dealing with pressures of school and family. I cannot concentrate. I do not know what I want for myself in terms of career or anything. I don't feel like I have much of a life, just an existence and I'm not very happy.

I do not sleep well at all. I have had lots of nightmares over the past few months - the most frightening thing about them is that they have been actual life experiences. I'm afraid of being a failure, of not being able to do anything well or that makes me feel good. I don't really know who I am: My life seems inseparable from my parents. I've tried so hard to live up to my parents' expectations and yet I never seem to be able to do that. I used to be good-natured and cheerful; I now feel like I'm upset all the time; I'm a volcano waiting to erupt.

Educating Patients About Schemas. The third step in the identification process is to educate patients about the nature of schemas. The therapist explains that a schema is an extremely strong belief about themselves that they learned at a very young age. The belief is so strong they simply assume it to be true. The therapist points out that a schema is different from most other types of thinking in the respect that it has tremendous emotional strength behind it. It has the strength of a lifetime of memories and of constant repetition to back it up.

Schemas are often central to patients' entire self-image and view of the world. Naturally, the schema is going to fight very hard for survival. It may feel very comfortable and even reassuring to patients to hold onto the schema, regardless of its negative consequences for their lives. We sometimes compare a schema to a comfortable old shoe that is not of much use anymore but feels too comfortable to throw out.

We explain to patients that we anticipate that they are going to distort information to maintain the schema, so they should not become discouraged because the schema is so slow to change. We are trying to prepare them for what the process of schema change is going to be like. We use the metaphor of a war and emphasize that we are going to have to do battle with the schema. We then usually suggest that patients read *Reinventing Your Life* (Young & Klosko, 1993), a self-help book based on the schema-focused approach, as well as the "Client's Guide to Schema-Focused Cognitive Therapy" (see Appendix D, pp. 79-90).

After explaining about the nature of schemas, the therapist reviews the Schema Questionnaire in detail with the patient. The therapist pays particular attention to items on which the patient scored high (5 or 6) by asking for examples to amplify and clarify the patient's responses. When possible, the therapist attempts to link SQ responses with presenting problems or with Life History Questionnaire responses in order to demonstrate the relevance of schemas to the patient's life.

Below are the schemas on which Carla scored high on the Schema Questionnaire. (These are based on an earlier version of the Questionnaire. For the most recent version see Appendix C, pp. 63-77).

1. *Dependence.* She mentioned that she could not separate her own life from her parents' life.

2. *Subjugation/Lack of Individuation.* Carla stated in her questionnaire and during the session that she put the needs of others ahead of her own, and that she would like to be able to think about herself more. She also mentioned not having a sense of identity, of not knowing what she wanted; and she noted the symptom of anger. These are all typical of patients with a subjugation schema, in which the issue is one of subjugating her own needs and her own identity in order to please other people.

3. *Fear of Losing Self-Control.* Carla mentioned that she pictured herself losing control, hurting others, and not being able to cope. These are typical fears reported by patients who are afraid that they are vulnerable to losing control.

4. *Incompetence/Failure.* Carla mentioned that she was afraid of being a failure, felt she made too many mistakes, and could not do anything right.

5.-8. *Abandonment, Defectiveness/Unlovability, Emotional Deprivation, and Social Undesirability.* These all seemed to be major themes for Carla. She mentioned a fear of being alone, a fear of losing people important to her, lonely images, being unlovable and undesirable, a sense of being lost, and feeling socially undesirable. Carla also indicated that she saw herself as unattractive and ugly.

23

9. *Unrelenting Standards.* Carla seemed to have considerable difficulty in setting reasonable expectations for herself, particularly in the realm of unrealistic achievement and responsibility. Carla mentioned that she was pushing herself but did not know why; that she should be good at everything she does; that she should strive for perfection; and that she wanted to have more balance between work and other areas. She identified working too hard as a problem behavior.

10. *Guilt/Punishment.* Finally, it appeared that Carla might be having difficulty with guilt/punishment. She mentioned in her Life History Questionnaire that she was trying to make someone understand her but "They're angry at me. They think I did something but I didn't." This is the typical thinking of patients with the guilt/punishment schema: that somehow they have done something wrong or are bad, and they anticipate being punished.

Triggering Schemas. Up to this point, the identification process has been primarily cognitive, that is, rational and intellectual. The next step is for the therapist to trigger schemas in an affective manner during the session and outside the session. By utilizing emotive techniques to trigger schemas, the therapist can test each of the schemas hypothesized during the first four steps to see whether or not it applies to the case. One can usually determine that a schema has been triggered when a high level of affect is aroused. The higher the level of affect, the more primary the schema is likely to be. Secondary schemas are generally less emotionally charged, and may not be triggered at all during this phase. There are a variety of strategies for triggering schemas:

Imagery. One extremely helpful technique is to ask patients to close their eyes and to report whatever images come to mind spontaneously. A variation of this technique is to ask the patient to get an image of a specific type of situation that the therapist believes, from previous data obtained from the patient, will trigger the schema. This, for example, could be a scene with a spouse or a parent.

Returning to our case example, Carla reported three images during her second therapy session. First, as she reported seeing the cafeteria in her high school, she began to feel very dizzy during the session. She said, "I'm not attached to my body. I'm not in control."

Her second image was of her parents and brother when she was a child. She reported that her parents looked very unhappy and were fighting about her brother. Her brother was not working enough in school and was not taking care of his room. While reporting this second image, Carla reported that her head was spinning, the noise was very loud, and her head was aching.

In her third image, she was alone in her room. She reported feeling cold and "closed up. There is nothing inside and nothing outside. I feel different, I'm out of control."

These images reinforced hypotheses formed earlier about Carla regarding specific schemas. The fear of losing self-control was evident in her reaction to the first image. The themes of failure and unrelenting standards were evident in the second image. The theme of being abandoned was apparent in the third image.

Current Events. A second technique for triggering schemas is to discuss upsetting events currently taking place in the patient's life. By asking the patient to discuss events that are distressing or that trigger strong feelings, and by inquiring about the meaning of those events, the therapist can get further information about schemas.

In the third session Carla reported getting extremely angry and anxious about her law school work. The anger, she said, was because, "I've got to wear this image because that's all the professors care about." Upon further questioning she mentioned that her whole life had involved wearing an image - being what other people wanted her to be, not what she felt like herself. When asked what she would be like if she was just herself, she responded that she did not know and could not find out so long as she was trying so hard to be what other people wanted her to be. This discussion of current problems, specifically the image she felt she had to "wear" at school, offered confirmation of the subjugation schema.

Past Memories. The third technique for eliciting schemas is to invite the patient to discuss memories and distressing experiences from the past. Recalling early childhood experiences, often through imagery, generates a high level of affect. These experiences, we presume, served to initiate the schema.

In the fourth session, the therapist asked Carla if she would discuss her parents and how she dealt with pressure when she was younger. She reported that her parents had always made decisions for her. As she began to talk about her daily routine as a youngster, she became increasingly agitated. She recalled that she was spending 9 hours doing homework every day by the age of 12. She was so afraid of failing in seventh grade that she had no life of her own. She also mentioned that during her teenage years she was afraid of growing up in front of her mother because it had been so painful to watch her adolescent brother fighting with her mother. She said, "I wanted to protect my mother." This discussion of the past offered further confirmation of the subjugation schema and the unrelenting standards schema.

Therapeutic Relationship. Another strategy for activating schemas is to discuss the therapeutic relationship - what analysts refer to as the transference. In schema-focused cognitive therapy, the therapist pays close attention to the therapeutic relationship, looking for events that seem to trigger schemas during the session. When these events arise, the therapist spends time discussing those aspects of the therapeutic relationship that are difficult for the patient.

During the second, third, and fourth months of therapy with Carla, considerable time was devoted to discussion of the therapeutic relationship. As early as the sixth session, Carla reported fearing that she would become dependent on the therapist and eventually would not be able to separate herself. She also reported that she wanted someone to be there for her but was afraid that he would leave her. Carla was asked to write more about these thoughts for homework. These are excerpts:

> So much of the time I am afraid of you - what you think, what you ask me. I pray all the time that somebody could really understand me and what I feel - especially since I don't - and that he'd never leave me alone. But I'm always alone
> . . . .
> It hurts so much to want somebody to care because it just never materializes. I feel like a thing that most of the time is a pain in the ass

and once in a while a convenience . . . I don't want to be alone.

These discussions about the therapeutic relationship further confirmed Carla's vulnerability to the abandonment, emotional deprivation, and defectiveness/unlovability schemas.

Books and Movies. Schemas can also be triggered by assigning books and films that are relevant to the hypothesized schemas. Books and movies have proven to be very powerful ways of activating schemas, which can then be discussed at the next session.

During the course of Carla's therapy, the therapist proposed several books or movies, including *Drama of the Gifted Child* by Alice Miller (1981), *Desert Bloom* (Corr, 1986), a film, and *Separation* by John Bowlby (1973). *Drama of the Gifted Child* was selected because it deals with the theme of a child subjugating her own needs to please a parent; *Separation*, because it deals specifically with the theme of abandonment; and *Desert Bloom*, because it deals with a young girl similar to Carla. As Carla described *Desert Bloom*: "The kid was trying so hard to please and the mother didn't understand the child. She was closed out of the family, just trying to keep the peace." Carla reported that she was fuming with anger and hostility after watching the movie. She reported similarly powerful emotional reactions to *Drama of the Gifted Child* and *Separation*.

Group Therapy. Group therapy is an excellent forum for triggering schemas that are interpersonal in nature. The therapist arranged for Carla to enter a group that was specifically focused on intimacy and interpersonal relationships. The other members of the group were dealing with similar issues of failure, abandonment, and subjugation. Each week Carla and the therapist would briefly review what had happened in the group that week, with particular emphasis on key moments or themes that triggered strong emotions for Carla.

During the first group session, Carla was completely immobilized and panicked and could say nothing. She reported that she was afraid her feelings would go out of control, that she would be attacked by the group, and that she felt ashamed of herself. She said, "No one can put up with me."

In a later group session she became extremely distressed when another group member spoke about being forced by parents to do things he did not want to do as a child. Carla commented to the therapist that "the only way to have contact is to live their way." This session set off an entire week in which her schema about her family controlling her and forcing her to do things their way was triggered. She felt continual anger and fear. These group experiences offered further support for the importance of the subjugation, fear of losing self-control, guilt/punishment, and defectiveness/unlovability schemas.

Dreams. Dreams are another helpful technique for eliciting schemas. In an early session, Carla reported having repeated nightmares. Each night she would dream that her mother was leaving her in a strange house, that her mother was very mad at her, and that she had not cleaned up properly. Dreams like this validated schemas of abandonment, emotional deprivation, defectiveness/unlovability, unrelenting standards, and incompetence/failure.

Homework. The final strategy for triggering schemas is to ask patients to do homework assignments in which they are asked to write about a specific schema-related topic or to keep a Daily Record of Dysfunctional Thoughts.

During the third month of therapy the therapist asked Carla to keep a diary in which she would write down her thoughts and feelings whenever she became particularly upset. One week she reported feeling panicky and nervous, afraid that she was losing her grip on everything. She wrote the following:

> I only want to be a good person. I want to be able to love and be loved back, and I don't want it to be taken away or have to give it up. I'm always making mistakes, hurting those who care for me the most.
>
> I'm just not as good as other people. Everyone is so disappointed and angry with me and I am too. I know other people hate me too, wish I were out of the way. I want somebody to hold me, but nobody is ever there. And even if someone were there, I wouldn't want to bother him.

In this diary excerpt, Carla poignantly conveys schemas related to abandonment, defectiveness/unlovability, emotional deprivation, guilt/punishment, and unrelenting standards.

Confronting Schema Avoidance. Most patients with personality disorders evidence some degree of schema avoidance. This schema avoidance is usually the patient's way of avoiding the high emotional intensity and unpleasantness that is experienced when a schema erupts. It is important to be able to recognize when the patient is having a symptom that is part of a schema and when the patient is experiencing a symptom that is primarily an avoidance of a schema.

Two characteristics seem to differentiate schema avoidance from the schema itself. When a patient experiences symptoms or emotions but cannot identify the content connected with them, this is usually typical of schema avoidance. In Carla's case, she would frequently feel anxious, sad, or angry, but not be able to report what she was anxious, sad, or angry about.

Another identifying characteristic of schema avoidance is the presence of somatic symptoms like dizziness, faintness, fever, depersonalization, and numbness, rather than "primary" emotions such as anger, fear, sadness, or guilt. Vague somatic symptoms are very often indications of schema avoidance.

In Carla's case, the therapist frequently observed that as soon as they began to discuss issues of abandonment, she would begin to report feeling very cold or dizzy. Sometimes she would depersonalize and not be able to go on with the sessions.

This was a particular problem during the third month of therapy. Carla would often become immobilized and be unable to speak for 20 minutes at a time because the material being dealt with was too painful for her to focus on. During these long stretches of silence, Carla would report that she did not know what she was thinking about, but had depersonalized or felt cold or dizzy and wanted to escape from the session.

These symptoms are all indications of schema avoidance. By examining the themes being discussed when the schema avoidance begins, it is often possible to deduce the areas in which core schemas are likely to be found.

When the therapist recognizes that schema avoidance is taking place, it is essential to push the patient to confront the thoughts, images, and emotions that are connected with the schema and not to run away from them. (This may not always be possible with more fragile, lower functioning patients.) This can be accomplished by discussing with the patient the pros and cons of looking at these upsetting issues.

With Carla, each time she would start to feel cold, depersonalized, or dizzy, the therapist would ask her what she was thinking about just before depersonalizing. When she said she could not remember, he would remind her what they were talking about and insist that she begin to talk about that issue again. He would also push her to focus on an image that he knew from previous experience might trigger the schema again. When Carla expressed the desire to escape, the therapist suggested to her that escaping would just prolong the process and would not allow them to examine the issues that were so important to her.

After repeated pushing and confrontation by the therapist, the patient is often able to refocus on the schema and begin once again to discuss the content connected with the schema. The therapist must help the patient see that the short-term pain of experiencing the schema will be outweighed by the long-term benefits of acknowledging the schema and working to change it.

Six months after the therapy had begun with Carla, most of the material connected with her schemas, including early memories and issues connected with the therapeutic relationship, had been discussed and experienced. Many of the somatic symptoms stopped completely. Specifically, the dizziness, faintness, coldness, fever, depersonalization, and numbness disappeared. Her primary emotions - namely fear, anger, sadness, and guilt - remained. Now she was able to identify the events in the past and present that triggered those feelings, and she could see how her interpretations of events in the past and present were related to these emotions.

Identifying Schema-Driven Behavior. The sixth step in identifying schemas is to recognize the schema-driven behaviors. As mentioned earlier in this guide, one of the reasons that early schemas are so often maladaptive is that patients develop self-defeating behavior patterns that reinforce the schemas. These schema-driven behaviors are the processes by which patients learn to cope with and adapt to their environment, based on the self-perceptions generated by the schemas. Each schema-driven behavior can be classified as: schema maintenance, schema avoidance, or schema compensation, depending on its function.

These behaviors simultaneously maintain the schema intact, allow the patient to avoid triggering the schema, and permit the patient to function in the world with as little distress as possible. Schema-driven behaviors, therefore, maintain an uneasy equilibrium for the patient. In this regard, they parallel the concept of neurosis: They are partially reinforced responses.

On the positive side, the patient avoids the painful affect connected to the schema and is usually able to function adequately in the world. On the negative side, the schema itself is never really changed, so the patient is always vulnerable to trigger events that threaten to disrupt the uneasy balance between coping and not coping. Furthermore, these behaviors often involve the avoidance of major life concerns, such as close relationships or a challenging career.

Identifying schema-driven behaviors requires a careful analysis of the patient's actual behaviors in specific problem areas. Once these schema-driven behaviors have been confirmed, the therapist presents them to the patient and obtains feedback.

Carla dealt with romantic relationships by avoiding them altogether, or by terminating them very quickly as soon as intimacy began. She developed this behavior as a way of coping with schemas about defectiveness/unlovability and abandonment. Carla was so convinced that she was undesirable, and that anyone she got close to would leave once they got to know her, that she saw no reason to pursue relationships and face certain abandonment.

Table 3 (p. 32) illustrates each of Carla's problem areas, the relevant schemas, and the schema-driven behaviors. It is important to note that more than one schema can be associated with each life area. Furthermore, a schema may be activated in one life area for a particular patient, yet not be activated in other problem domains.

Conceptualizing the Patient in Schema Terms. Steps seven and eight both involve conceptualizing the patient in schema terms. First, the therapist must link up the material obtained through the procedures described above, and then demonstrate the connection between schemas, emotions, current trigger events, the therapeutic relationship, and origins from the past.

TABLE 3: **CASE EXAMPLE ILLUSTRATING RELATIONSHIP BETWEEN PROBLEM AREAS, SCHEMAS, AND SCHEMA-DRIVEN BEHAVIORS**

PROBLEM AREAS	SCHEMAS	SCHEMA-DRIVEN BEHAVIORS
Romantic Relationships	Abandonment Unlovability Social Undesirability	Avoids men most of the time. Terminates relationships as soon as she begins to feel close. (Schema avoidance)
School Performance	Subjugation Incompetence/ Failure Unrelenting Standards	Studies constantly. No time for pleasure. Does whatever professors expect. (Schema maintenance)
Family Relationships	All of Her Schemas	Constantly tries to meet parents' expectations. Suppresses own emotions and needs. (Schema maintenance)
Therapy Relationship	Abandonment/Loss Unlovability Emotional Deprivation Social Undesirability Shame/Embarrassment Fear of Losing Self-Control	Constantly tries to please therapist. Thanks therapist inordinately. Apologizes for not being a good patient. Keeps head down during sessions. Tries to suppress anger and crying during sessions. Worries inordinately about therapist abandoning her, especially when he goes on vacation. (Schema maintenance)

Once the therapist is able to identify these schemas and to see how they manifest themselves in the past and present, the therapist summarizes these conclusions for the patient and asks for feedback. These schemas are then fine-tuned until the patient and therapist agree that the formulation is accurate. Table 4 (pp. 34-35) describes the schemas as the therapist summarized them for Carla, after obtaining feedback from her.

The final step is for the therapist to distinguish among primary, secondary, and associated schemas. To do this, the therapist must understand how all the relevant schemas interrelate.

The therapist's first objective is to identify the one or two core, or primary, schemas; these generally serve as the initial targets for the change procedures outlined in the next section. These core schemas can be isolated by paying close attention to events triggering high levels of affect, to the most serious and enduring life problems, and to the early origins of the patient's emotional distress.

Primary schemas are identified through three criteria. The first is that a primary schema usually triggers the highest level of emotion. The second is that a primary schema is almost always closely linked to the most distressing, pervasive, and enduring life problems experienced by the patient. Third, the core schemas are usually closely tied to the patient's most serious developmental problems with parents, siblings, or peers during the early years of life.

After identifying the primary schemas, the therapist looks for other schemas that are *associated* with each primary schema. An associated schema is one that can be best explained by reference to a primary schema. For example, with Carla, the fear of losing self-control schema was directly related to the anger generated by constantly subjugating her needs to others. In schema language, the fear of losing self-control was an associated schema, related to the primary schema of subjugation.

After delineating primary and associated schemas, the therapist identifies the secondary schemas. These schemas are relatively independent of the primary schemas, and seem to be of lower priority and salience. These secondary schemas are targeted for change later in the treatment process.

Table 5 (p. 36) illustrates the differentiation of primary, secondary, and associated schemas in the case of Carla.

CHANGING SCHEMAS

Overview. In this final section, four major types of intervention will be outlined: emotive, interpersonal, cognitive, and behavioral. In general, the emotive techniques are stressed at the beginning of treatment to "loosen up" the schemas and make them more flexible for change.

TABLE 4: CASE EXAMPLE ILLUSTRATING RELATIONSHIP BETWEEN SCHEMAS, EMOTIONS, TRIGGERS, AND ORIGINS

SCHEMAS	EMOTIONS	CURRENT TRIGGERS
1. Subjugation	Anger	Having to conform in law school. Having to follow parents' advice on financial issues.
2. Fear of Losing Self-Control	Panic (about anger)	Dealing with parents in any way triggers past resentments.
3. Guilt/Punishment	Guilt Fear of Punishment	Not being home to take care of parents. Using up parents' money for therapy. Criticizing parents in session.
4. Incompetence/ Failure and Unrelenting Standards	Anxiety Anger at Self	Fear about not working hard enough at school. Continually striving for excellence.
5. Abandonment Unlovability Emotional Deprivation	Lonely Sad Scared	Spending extended periods of time alone.
6. Social Undesirability Shame/Embarrassment	Sad Ashamed	Thinking about dating men or going to a party.

(Table 4 continued on next page)

Interpersonal techniques are emphasized throughout treatment with patients who display their schemas in the therapeutic relationship ("transference"). This is particularly important for patients with core schemas in the connectedness domain, including emotional deprivation, abandonment, and mistrust.

Cognitive techniques are utilized next to systematize the process of schema change. Patients are taught cognitive techniques that enable them to fight schemas each time they arise outside the session. They learn how to battle their emotional beliefs persistently with rational arguments. Patients also learn how schemas distort infor-

TABLE 4 (Continued)

TRIGGERS IN THERAPY RELATIONSHIP	EARLY ORIGINS OF SCHEMAS (HYPOTHESIZED)
1. Always defers to therapist.	Parents became very angry whenever she asserted her own needs. Patient observed parents fighting with brother when brother tried to become independent.
2. When therapist goes away on vacations (triggers anger and and sadness).	Rage at parents for mistreating her. Parents punished her whenever she showed anger or sadness.
3. Fear that she is wasting therapist's time. Crying uncontrollably in sessions (whenever she cannot answer therapist's questions).	Punished by parents whenever she made mistakes or cried.
4. Fear that she is not getting better fast enough or is not a good enough patient.	Parents set impossibly high standards and got angry whenever she failed to meet them.
5. The end of a therapy session. Therapist goes on vacation.	Parents left her alone with nurses throughout infancy and childhood. Mother would walk away and not talk to her when she cried or did something wrong.
6. Keeping her head down so therapist will not see her "ugly face."	Mother harped on her physical flaws, especially weight problems.

mation and thus reinforce the strength of beliefs that otherwise would seem illogical.

The final stage is behavioral change. This is usually the longest phase, because it involves changing long-term self-defeating behavioral patterns that have become deeply entrenched. It is often easier to alter emotions and beliefs than to change these behaviors, such as patterns of partner selection or intimacy.

Regardless of which phase of treatment the patient is undergoing, we have found it essential that schemas be challenged *when they are triggered*, that is, when affective arousal relevant to the schema has been activated in the patient. Even during the cognitive phase, discussing sche-

TABLE 5: CASE ILLUSTRATION OF PRIMARY, SECONDARY, AND ASSOCIATED SCHEMAS

SCHEMAS	SCHEMA RANKING	ASSOCIATED SCHEMAS	EXPLANATION
1. Subjugation	Primary	Fear of Losing Self-Control Guilt/Punishment Incompetence/ Failure Unrelenting Standards	Subjugation is primary. Patient was made to feel guilty and bad when she asserted her own needs. Nature of subjugation involved meeting parents' high standards for achievement. Patient was made to feel like a failure if she was less than perfect.
2. Abandonment	Primary	Emotional Deprivation Unlovability	Abandonment is primary. Parents left her alone so often as an infant that she never developed a stable sense of attachment. Absence of nurturance contributed to feeling of deprivation, associated with core fear of abandonment. Child attributed abandonment to being unlovable.
3. Shame/ Embarrassment	Secondary	Social Undesirability	Patient was made to feel ashamed of her appearance by mother's continual criticism. This later led to a feeling of being unattractive and undesirable in social settings with peers.

mas in the abstract or intellectually is rarely as powerful as questioning them in the presence of affect.

For example, if a particular patient has an abandonment schema, the therapist will probably make more headway with the issue during a session just before going away for a vacation than at some other time. Just before the therapist's vacation, the patient is most likely to be angry, anxious, or depressed in session. The schema will probably be activated and therefore more accessible.

36

The remainder of the guide will be devoted to elaborating on the four types of interventions, drawing again on the case of Carla for illustration.

Emotive Techniques. There are a number of helpful techniques available to the therapist to change schemas at an emotional level for the patient. Most of these techniques are drawn from gestalt therapy, and many involve triggering schemas in the session so that greater change can take place.

One of these techniques is to *create imaginary dialogues* with the patient's parents. The therapist usually asks patients to close their eyes and try to get an image of their mother or father. After obtaining a brief description of the event they are picturing, the therapist will suggest that they carry on a dialogue with the parent, in which they tell the parent exactly what they want and feel. Sometimes patients can alternately play themselves, then their parents. At other times, the therapist will play one of the roles while the patient plays the other. The therapist asks patients to keep their eyes closed so that the realism gained through imagery is not lost. By playing themselves as they would have liked to respond to their parents, patients usually begin to change their beliefs about themselves. They can see more clearly the role of their parents in perpetuating the schemas, and, by talking back to their parents and defending themselves, patients usually observe that their schemas start to weaken.

A second useful technique is *emotional catharsis.* Gestalt therapists often stress the importance of unfinished emotional business. Chronic patients often have unexpressed anger and rage based on early life experiences. Frequently, they also have other painful issues (such as early deprivation or loss) that they have not yet acknowledged and "grieved" for. When the therapist raises these issues through imagery, role playing, or current life experiences, and encourages the patient to express ("ventilate") the associated feelings, the schemas associated with these feelings often change.

In Carla's case, for example, there were two areas in which she needed emotional catharsis. The first involved her anger toward her parents for their mistreatment and neglect of her when she was a child. The therapist had her write a letter to her parents listing all of the ways in which she felt she had been mistreated, with specific examples of each type of neglect, but he asked her to wait until he checked with her parents before mailing it. The therapist prepared the parents in advance by touching on some of the issues that might come up, and by asking them whether they could handle an extremely critical letter from their daughter. Both parents felt they could handle it, so he asked Carla to mail her letter.

It seemed important to complete this process of encouraging Carla to ventilate some of her *justifiable* anger so that she could then start letting go of it. The therapist then arranged an extremely successful family session in which her mother apologized and acknowledged that she had been negligent in all the specific ways Carla had described in her letter. Carla evidenced an enormous mood improvement after this experience. After ventilating her anger, Carla began to see that she was not really the terrible person in the family she had been led to believe she was.

Interpersonal Techniques. One of the most potent methods for changing schemas is through the *therapeutic relationship* itself. The therapist is constantly alert for indications that patients' schemas are being activated in relationship to the therapist. When this happens, the therapist helps patients test the reality of their beliefs through direct interaction between the therapist and patient. This often involves self-disclosure on the part of the therapist to correct patient distortions.

During one session Carla told the therapist that she thought that he viewed her as physically repulsive. The therapist used this as an opportunity to challenge her shame/embarrassment schema. He utilized the Point-Counterpoint technique (described later). Most of the session was devoted to a dialogue in which she told him her negative physical image of herself, and he corrected this view as he saw her physically. In other words, she played her negative schema while the therapist provided the alternate point of view. They later changed roles and she had to argue against her schema, that he found her repulsive. By the end of the session, Carla could see that she was operating on the basis of an early schema that was leading her to predict, inaccurately, what the therapist thought about her.

Another interpersonal strategy is for the therapist to *provide a therapeutic relationship that counteracts early maladaptive schemas.* In some respects, we are advocating a reparenting role for the therapist. With some patients like Carla, we urge therapists to try to find out what needs of the child did not get met and to try to meet them to a reasonable degree - although not to a degree that would make the therapist angry or resentful.

For example, if the patient has suffered a great deal of emotional deprivation, the therapist can try, within limits, to be nurturing and caring. A knowledge of each patient's schemas can guide the therapist in deciding what aspects of the reparenting process might be especially important. One patient might need a lot of autonomy, another discipline, another reassurances of competence, and still another patient may need the therapist to set lower expectations for performance. The reparenting process can provide one of the most powerful mechanisms for invalidating the patient's schemas.

For Carla, it was extremely important for her to see that the therapist was there for her in a consistent way when she needed him, that he was not punitive or critical of her, that he cared for her (within the confines of a therapeutic relationship), and that he liked her. Carla said to the therapist during the sixth month of treatment: "I know that you're there for me. This is the first time anyone has been, and I'm afraid of losing you." She also wrote the following flashcard (a technique that will be discussed in more detail later), in response to her schema that she would be abandoned and left alone forever:

Jeff won't leave me. Jeff will help me find someone I love who will keep loving me. I am lovable. I have to learn how to choose men who can get close and make commitments. I will not be alone forever. I can take steps to be loved.

Another interpersonal strategy is to arrange group therapy experiences for patients, in order to provide an environment that will counteract schemas and help break self-defeating interpersonal patterns.

As mentioned earlier, the therapist arranged for Carla to participate in group therapy. The group served to highlight some of the positive experiences Carla would be able to have with other people. One group member told her how helpful and perceptive she was. Carla's individual therapist relayed to her the opinion of the group therapist that he used her as the thermometer for the group; she could feel whatever the group was feeling.

This positive feedback represented evidence she could draw on that was contrary to her schemas.

Cognitive Techniques. Many of the techniques drawn from short-term cognitive therapy can be adapted to schema work. We will devote considerable time to these strategies in order to emphasize the value of cognitive techniques in changing deeper structures.

Review Evidence in Support of the Schemas. Before trying to change a schema, it is very important to elicit all of the information that the patient uses to support it. Patients have a lifetime of evidence which they can draw on to support the validity of their schemas. To elicit this evidence, the therapist first does a life review. The therapist reviews the origins of the schema in childhood by evoking any memories the patient recalls that might be relevant to the schema. The therapist then traces the schema as it developed and was reinforced through adolescence and adulthood.

The therapist can also ask the patient to play "devil's advocate," defending the schema. The therapist introduces this technique by saying: "I want you to defend the schema, while I try to show you why I think the schema is not true. Make the best case you possibly can in support of the schema, and be sure to give me as many examples as possible to validate it."

Returning to our case illustration again, the therapist asked Carla to defend her abandonment and unlovability schemas. She gave him three basic arguments in support of her unlovability. First, her parents and brother were constantly angry at her and critical of her when she was a child; therefore she must not be very lovable. Second, she had been rejected by three boyfriends. Finally, she was left alone a lot. In the next stage of schema change, the therapist begins to cast doubt on this evidence.

Examine the Supporting Evidence Critically. The goal in this stage is to go through each piece of evidence that the patient offers in support of the schema and to try to discover some other way of viewing that same information so that it does not really prove the schema. The therapist can discredit the evidence in a variety of ways. One method is to use collaborative empiricism or guided discovery to help patients see for themselves that the schema is invalid. At other times the therapist will have to use a more confrontational style, depending on how strong the schema maintenance processes seem to be.

In working with early schemas, the therapist is continually working to find a balance between empathizing with the patient for the pain brought on by the schema, and confronting the patient with evidence that discredits the schema. If the therapist is too confrontational, the patient will ignore the counterarguments advanced by the therapist on the grounds that the therapist does not really understand how the patient feels.

One method for invalidating evidence is to *discount early family experiences as reflecting the maladaptive standards and expectations of their parents.* We emphasize that these parental standards do not generalize to teachers, bosses, friends, and so on, outside of the patients' home. Other family evidence can be discounted by pointing out the psychological maladjustment of each parent, of the marital couple, or of the family system. The therapist emphasizes that children are often assigned roles in a family that are not in the children's best interest, yet may serve a psychological need for one or both of the parents. These roles do not reflect any inherent flaws in the children, but rather they are the result of distorted family dynamics. The therapist often examines each family member individually, with the patients' help, until the therapist can shift patients to a more realistic perspective on their early family life. By the end of this process, the therapist hopes that patients will experience sadness or anger about what happened to them in their childhood, yet not view these early experiences as proof of some inherent unlovability, flaw, incompetence, or badness.

In Carla's case, she and the therapist concluded, after examining each of the family members, that her whole family was living a lie. Below are some of the specific conclusions they reached about each of her family members.

Carla's mother was denying her own need for other people. She could not express positive feelings even with her husband. She valued her career over her children. She was cold to everyone, not just to the patient. She was a perfectionist, who considered the children to be a nuisance interfering with her career. Carla concluded that her mother really did not single her out for coldness and criticism, since she treated her husband and her son the same way.

The father, she concluded, was not getting his needs met from her mother, and he turned inappropriately to the patient to get his needs met. He then got angry when the patient would not give him enough support and affection. His demands were interfering with her need to individuate. Like the mother, her father was a perfectionist. He had a terrible temper which he frequently took out on both children. Carla concluded that she was wrong in believing that her father was making realistic demands on her and that she was too inadequate to meet them. Rather she came to understand that her father was trying to get his own needs met inappropriately through her.

Finally, the therapist arranged for a joint therapy session with the patient and her brother. The brother confirmed that he had resented Carla because, even as a teenager, he was asked by his parents to take care of Carla all the time because the parents were never at home. Carla recognized that it was not her fault that she was a nuisance to her older brother. The problem was that the parents were making unreasonable demands on the brother, which placed Carla in the middle. Carla then became the scapegoat for the brother's frustration at not being able to spend time with his own friends.

A second strategy for discrediting evidence is to demonstrate to patients that, because of their schema-driven behaviors, they have never really given the schema a fair test. Remember that schema-driven behaviors are designed to keep the schemas intact while helping patients avoid situations that might trigger the schema.

Carla's second argument to prove she was unlovable was her view that three boyfriends had rejected her. To discount this evidence, she and the therapist had to review each of the three relationships with great care. They were soon able to identify her pattern of schema maintenance and avoidance behaviors: In each instance, she had chosen an unavailable boyfriend who was bound to leave. In one case it was a man who was visiting her city only for the winter; she met another man while she was traveling overseas shortly before she had to return to America; and in the third case, the man was a foreign student who would soon be going back to Denmark. Furthermore, with each of these men, it was Carla who distanced herself whenever the man tried to get close. Thus, even though the men may ultimately have been the ones who left, it was Carla who initiated the distance. Carla and the therapist agreed that the schema had never really been tested because she had used so many maneuvers to avoid becoming fully engaged in and committed to relationships that might trigger the schema.

Through this process, the therapist carefully examines patients' supporting evidence, pointing out ways in which patients have misconstrued past situations so that the schema is repeatedly confirmed. By the end of this stage of schema change, patients have begun to get some distance from their schemas. They are beginning to wonder if the schema may be a disastrous myth they have been perpetuating. Nevertheless, the schema still feels more powerful than the disconfirming evidence that they are only beginning to accumulate.

Review Evidence Contradicting the Schema. By this point, the therapist and patient have discredited the *negative* information which the patient uses to prove the schema. Now the therapist has to build up all of the *positive* information about the patient that will directly contradict the schema. In Carla's case, this included evidence that she is an effective person, ways in which she does take responsibility, areas of competence and success, and examples of mutually satisfying friendships in which she is valued for being herself. Keep in mind, however, that eliciting this positive information may prove much more difficult than eliciting the negative information. The selective forgetting of positive information is part of the schema maintenance processes that are operating continuously in the patient.

Illustrate How the Patient Discounts Contradictory Evidence. It is a basic premise of schema theory that the patient will actively discount evidence contradictory to the schema. This discounting is part of the schema maintenance process. In this phase of schema change, the therapist must demonstrate to the patient how this mechanism of discounting operates.

One excellent technique for doing this is the Point-Counterpoint (P-CP) technique. Point-Counterpoint can be practiced either aloud in the session or as part of a homework assignment. (The "devil's advocate" technique mentioned .earlier is a variation of Point-Counterpoint.) The therapist introduces P-CP by asking the patient to play the schema. The therapist takes the role of the healthy side. They have a debate back and forth in which the therapist makes a point in the patient's support, then the patient discounts it according to the schema, then the therapist responds to the discounting, and so forth. They then trade roles; the therapist plays the patient's schema and the patient plays the healthy part. When P-CP is used as a homework assignment, the patient plays both parts: the schema and the adaptive point of view.

In using this technique, it usually becomes obvious quickly that the patient has no difficulty whatsoever playing the role of the schema. This is understandable, since the schema represents the patient's core beliefs throughout lifetime. The patient can see how skillfully any positive evidence contrary to the schema can be discounted. However, when asked to play the healthy, adaptive view, the patient generally gets stuck almost immediately. Often the patient is unable to repeat what the therapist said just 2 minutes earlier to contradict the schema.

This discrepancy between the patient's ease at playing the schema and the enormous difficulty in responding rationally to the schema is often a very powerful lesson. The patient can now see how hard the schema will fight to maintain itself, even when the evidence to the contrary is overpowering. By continuing to repeat this exercise session after session, and through homework assignments, the patient becomes better and better at fighting the schema. The patient observes how the schema negates positive information, and then learns to reclaim the positive evidence through reason and logic.

An important variation of this technique is to have the patient get angry at the schema. With this variation, the therapist provokes the patient by playing the schema in its most extreme, unyielding form. The patient tries to do battle with the schema by getting angry and refusing to give in to it. The addition of emotion to the P-CP technique often makes this adaptation even more effective. Getting angry at the schema seems to create even more distance between the healthy part of the patient and the maladaptive schema.

Below is an example of a P-CP homework assignment that Carla completed. The therapist had suggested that she base the assignment on the positive feedback she was getting while working with children.

+ : I'm very loving and giving when I feel safe.
- : But I'm only that way because I need people.
+ : It may be true that I need people, but that's certainly not the only reason that I'm loving. I sincerely empathize with people and don't want to hurt them.
- : But somehow I only end up hurting them anyway.
+ : I don't hurt them, but they hurt themselves. And not everyone involved with me ends up getting hurt, just my family. They're screwed up. I was their scapegoat when things went wrong.

Carla takes the positive evidence and discounts it; but then she tries to reclaim the positive evidence by countering her negating of the positive. This process goes back and forth until she can end the exercise on a positive statement.

Below is another example of P-CP related to Carla's schemas about abandonment, emotional deprivation, and unlovability:

- : I feel detached from people. I feel lonely.
+ : But I don't feel lonely when I'm at my work. Already over the past 3 months I've met new people who are receptive to me. I know the staff really likes me and cares about me and is happy to have me around.
- : I feel lonely outside of work though.
+ : It takes time to build friendships. It'll take time before I really feel secure again with a new group of people. I've already done a lot to change my life with Jeff's help, and I just have to be patient and keep working at it. I can't give up.

Again we see her struggling with the schema. Each time, there is a negative schema trying to prove that she is bad and unlovable; but, as the therapy progresses, there is also another side gradually growing stronger, a weak voice initially that is trying to see herself in a positive light.

Develop Flashcards that Contradict the Schemas. One of the most effective techniques for changing early schemas is the constant repetition of rational responses, especially whenever the schema is being activated. One of the simplest methods for providing this rehearsal and practice is to develop one or more flashcards for each of the major schemas. The flashcard is simply an index card, usually developed jointly by the patient and the therapist. It should incorporate the most powerful evidence and counterarguments against the schema itself. The evidence on the flashcards should include several specific instances when the schema was untrue. Patients should be encouraged to carry the flashcards with them wherever they go, and to pull them out whenever a relevant schema has been triggered.

In the flashcard that follows, Carla addresses her schema that she is a bad, selfish person who is not deserving of love:

> In a safe environment, I am loving and caring. I try to be giving and generous with all people, but most of all with children. Overall, I try to make people happy: I'm sensitive to people's needs and wishes, and I do everything I can to respect and satisfy them . . . .

A second flashcard responds to Carla's schema that she is unlovable because her mother was so cold toward her:

> My mother cannot love me or anyone because she denies her needs for others. She's afraid of being dependent on someone else, of being controlled, and of ultimately getting hurt - like she was hurt as a child . . . She and the people who love her suffer.

These flashcards almost always prove invaluable in making the slow transition from intellectual understanding to emotional acceptance of more adaptive thinking patterns.

Challenge the Schema Whenever It Is Activated During the Therapy Session or Outside the Session. A crucial aspect of schema-focused therapy is constant practice, as mentioned above in the discussion of flashcards. Every time we see the schema arising during the session, we point it out and help the patient to counteract it. Every time it comes up outside the session, we instruct the patient to write down what happened and either develop a new rational response or locate a flashcard from their "deck" of cards that might be relevant to the schema.

Behavioral Techniques. The next step in changing schemas is to *change schema-driven behaviors.* This involves pushing the patient to change long-term behavior patterns that have reinforced the schemas for most of the patient's lifetime.

For example, early on in Carla's treatment, the therapist identified a schema avoidance behavior that effectively kept men at a distance. Carla wrote the following flashcard to clarify the dysfunctional aspect of this pattern with men:

> I feel unlovable because I was left alone a lot as a child and was yelled at all the time. Because I felt unlovable, I avoided close contact with men, or I chose men who I knew could not make a commitment. By doing this, I have been able to continually confirm my negative schema that I am unlovable.

The therapist worked with Carla to select men who were more truly available emotionally for her, and to develop better intimacy skills in the earlier stages so that she would not distance herself inappropriately.

There were many other areas as well in which the therapist helped Carla change her maladaptive schema-driven behaviors: He urged her to express anger toward her parents, which she had never done before. The therapist urged her to choose a new career based on her interests, which involved working with children. This was extremely important, because it was the first time in her life that she had ever been allowed to do anything that she loved and that she had chosen because she wanted it, not to please someone else.

Carla began expressing her emotions in session much more freely. As she did this, her emotional symptoms like numbness, coldness, and dizziness disappeared. Soon in a session she could cry, get angry, be nervous, and not feel that she had to hide it from the therapist. She could look at him without hiding her face. She stopped apologizing to him and thanking him for normal therapy sessions.

Finally, she learned to balance work with pleasure. Carla was no longer working 20 hours a day, and she had more realistic expectations of herself in school. She was no longer pushing herself to be the very best in her class.

Another strategy for bringing about behavioral change is to *make environmental changes when necessary.* It is very important to make changes in the patient's environment when the therapist believes that these changes can either make therapy more productive or can give the patient enough "breathing room" to focus on the therapy. We will sometimes work with spouses conjointly. We might encourage patients to move away from their homes temporarily, reduce work responsibilities temporarily, try out new hobbies or athletic activities, or initiate new relationships and friendships.

In the case of Carla, the therapist recommended a number of environmental changes. First, he urged her to stop her schooling temporarily, because she seemed too unstable to deal with both the therapy and her severe work pressures. He also supported her desire to work with children. The therapist also did a lot of work to strengthen her relationship with her brother while simultaneously having her cut off all contact with her parents except for the family sessions during the early phases of treatment. Therefore, it was necessary to make a number of specific environmental changes in order to enable Carla to make maximum use of the schema-focused cognitive therapy.

Carla had expressed an interest in working with children earlier in the treatment, but had dismissed it on the grounds that her parents would not approve and that it would not be financially practical. The therapist reasoned that, if she could make this life change, she might get evidence contradicting several schemas: She would not be subjugating her needs to her parents; she would be able to succeed at something she valued; she might form connections with children and other counselors; and she might even gain insight into how parental upbringing can affect the self-confidence of children.

The therapist suggested that she find a setting where she could work with children who were being abused or mistreated. The camp proved to be an extremely powerful experience. First, Carla could see how successful she was at working with these children, that she was very loving toward them, and that they reciprocated. Second, she started to observe many parallels in her own childhood as she observed interactions between these children and their parents. Carla could clearly see that these were not bad children, they simply had neglectful parents. These associations stimulated enormous rage toward her parents. This rage increased her belief that perhaps her schema was not true, that her parents had been unfair to her and, in fact, had mistreated her.

SUMMARY

Schema-focused cognitive therapy differs from short-term cognitive therapy in a number of respects:

1. There is less guided discovery and more confrontation.
2. There is much greater use of the therapeutic relationship as a vehicle of change.
3. There is much more resistance to change. Therefore, the therapy is lengthier.
4. The level of affect is much higher during schema-focused sessions.
5. The therapist is much more concerned with identifying and overcoming cognitive and behavioral avoidance.
6. Schema-focused cognitive therapy devotes considerably more time to the childhood origins of schemas and to emotive techniques surrounding these early issues.

At the same time, the schema-focused approach retains most of the important elements that differentiate Beck's approach from more traditional psychoanalytic or client-centered therapies.

1. The therapist is much more active.
2. The change techniques are much more systematic.
3. There is a strong emphasis on self-help homework assignments.
4. The therapeutic relationship is collaborative rather than neutral.
5. The schema-focused approach is much more rapid and direct than conventional psychotherapy.
6. The therapist uses an empirical approach insofar as the analysis of evidence is a critical aspect of schema change.

Schema-focused cognitive therapy, therefore, can be viewed as a significant extension of cognitive therapy, integrating techniques from other approaches to meet the special therapeutic requirements of difficult patients with longer-term personality disorders, and those with chronic anxiety or depression.

APPENDICES

APPENDIX A: HYPOTHESIZED
ORIGINS OF SCHEMAS

In considering the origin of these schemas, we have observed four primary tasks that we believe the child must negotiate in order to develop in a healthy manner. These four tasks are autonomy; connectedness; worthiness; and reasonable expectations and realistic limits. It seems that all of the schemas we have identified are developed when parents, siblings, or peers make it difficult for the child to achieve one or more of these four objectives.

Biology and Temperament. It should be noted that biology and temperament undoubtedly play some role in the development of some of these schemas. For example, a child who is especially anxious by nature may have more difficulty moving from dependence to autonomy. Similarly, a child who is shy by disposition may be more prone to developing the social isolation schema. The child's ability to negotiate each of the developmental tasks outlined below may in part be determined by a child's innate temperament, in combination with the parenting styles and social influences to which he or she is exposed. For the remainder of this section, however, we will assume that the child does not present any exceptional biological traits that would significantly interfere with the mastery of each task. The emphasis, therefore, will be on the roles of parents, siblings, and peers in the development of EMS's.

Autonomy. Autonomy is the sense that one can function independently in the world, without continual support from others. Autonomous individuals can express their individual needs, interests, preferences, opinions, and feelings. They have a sense of integrity and control within themselves, physically, mentally, and psychologically. Finally, autonomous people believe that their environment is relatively safe, and they are not hypervigilant to threat.

In order to develop a sense of themselves as autonomous individuals, children need parents who encourage them to express their own autonomous needs and to act on these needs without undue restriction, punishment, or withdrawal of support. Children need encouragement to function independently without excessive help from the parents. They need assurance that they are healthy, robust individuals, and that the world is relatively safe. They should be given the freedom to express the full range of emotions, including anger. Finally, children should be assigned responsibilities to undertake on their own.

When parents fail to provide an environment that encourages autonomy, one of the four schemas related to autonomy could develop. These include vulnerability to harm and illness, fear of losing self-control, subjugation and lack of individuation, and pervasive feelings of dependency. These often arise when parents overprotect their children; for example, by continually warning them of exaggerated dangers and risks. Autonomy problems can arise when children observe parents worrying continually and unnecessarily, or when children are not given enough independent responsibility. Many parents jump in when children are having even minimal difficulty. The opposite extreme can also lead to problems with dependency: when children are rarely helped to do anything and receive little guidance or direction. It appears that either extreme - either doing everything for children or providing too little for them - can lead to difficulties with autonomy.

Another possible origin of these autonomy schemas can be lack of encouragement when children begin to express their own needs, interests, desires, or opinions. Many parents are overcontrolling and create an environment where their needs take precedence over their children's. A final problem in the autonomy realm is when parents discourage or punish children for expressing their feelings, particularly anger, or when parents do not model the expression of emotions around their children. Any of these parental difficulties can make it difficult for children to have the secure sense that they can express their own needs and feelings without fear of reprisal.

Connectedness. Connectedness is the sense that one is connected to other people in a stable, enduring, and trusting manner. One form of connectedness involves intimacy: close emotional ties to others. This is enhanced when individuals see themselves as lovable and when they trust the motives of others.

A second form of connectedness involves social integration: a sense of belonging and fitting into a group of friends, family, and community. Social integration is promoted when individuals believe they are socially desirable and skilled, and when they feel similar to other people.

In order to develop a sense of connectedness, children need reliable love, nurturance, and dependable mothering and fathering. This leads children to feel cared for. Children also need empathy from the parents for the children's feelings. This leads to a sense of being understood. Children need a secure family environment without excessive fighting. They need equal love and attention in relationship to their brothers and sisters. Parents should encourage children to socialize with other children. Finally, to develop the sense of connectedness, children need to have successful experiences socializing with peers individually and in groups, throughout childhood and adolescence. When children do not have this kind of secure environment, with love, empathy, attention, respect, and positive social experiences, they are prone to the schemas related to disconnectedness: social isolation/alienation, emotional deprivation, abandonment/loss, and mistrust.

Children are prone to developing these schemas when they do not receive enough love, affection, respect, or attention from their parents. Sometimes this happens when parents die or leave the home permanently, or when children are frequently left alone during very early years. Disconnectedness can also develop when children are rejected by other children or for some other reason are unable to become a member of a peer group. These schemas of connectedness can also develop when children lack qualities that are considered highly desirable for social attractiveness to the opposite sex, or when they do not have interests that are traditionally gender appropriate. Finally, disconnectedness can arise when children are abused, cheated, lied to, or beaten up by either parents or peers.

Worthiness. Worthiness is the sense that one is lovable, competent, acceptable, and desirable to others, and that one is worthy of the attention, love, and respect of others.

In order to develop a sense of worthiness, children need the love and respect of parents and siblings, and the social acceptance of peers. When children do not receive enough respect, love, and acceptance, and when they receive excessive criticism or punishment, they are prone to the schemas related to unworthiness: defectiveness/unlovability, social undesirability, incompetence/failure, guilt/punishment, and shame/embarrassment.

Reasonable Expectations and Realistic Limits. Reasonable expectations means having the capacity to set realistic, achievable standards for oneself and others, especially in the realms of performance and achievement. Realistic limits refers to the capacity to discipline oneself, to control one's impulses, and to take the needs of others into account, all to an appropriate degree.

It is important for children to develop a sense of limits. This is best accomplished by providing an environment that is neither too demanding nor too permissive. Children benefit from realistic limits on their behavior so they can learn self-control and concern for others. Parents can communicate the message that their children are not perfect and do not need to be perfect to be loved and fully accepted. Parents can help their children come to accept their own limitations. Finally, children need to learn a realistic sense of obligation to others. Children should neither be encouraged to be too selfish nor too self-sacrificing.

The unrelenting standards schema develops when children are asked to do more than they can reasonably complete and are taught that whatever they accomplish is not enough. These parents place a higher priority on achievement than on happiness. Children often feel that the only way they can earn the love of such parents is by achieving at an extremely high level.

The entitlement/insufficient limits schema arises when children are overindulged by parents; praised inordinately for accomplishments; allowed to do whatever they want, without regard for the needs of others; not taught that relationships involve sharing and reciprocity; and not taught how to deal with defeat or frustration. These children may be told that they are special and few limits are set.

To summarize, then, children have four primary tasks: autonomy; connectedness; worthiness; and reasonable expectations and realistic limits. When the parents and the social environment are optimal, children develop in a healthy way in all four areas. However, when the parental or social environment is not optimal, children are vulnerable to developing early maladaptive schemas in one or more of these core areas. These schemas then persist over a lifetime and become organizing principles for patients' emotional and behavioral functioning.

APPENDIX B:
EARLY MALADAPTIVE SCHEMAS
(Revised Schema Listing; January, 1994)*

DISCONNECTION AND REJECTION

(Expectation that one's needs for security, safety, stability, nurturance, empathy, sharing of feelings, acceptance, and respect will not be met in a predictable manner. Typical family origin is detached, explosive, unpredictable, rejecting, punitive, unforgiving, withholding, inhibited, or abusive.)

1. *Abandonment/Instability.* The perceived *instability* or *unreliability* of those available for support and connection.

   Involves the sense that significant others will not be able to continue providing emotional support, connection, strength, or practical protection because they are emotionally unstable and unpredictable (e.g., angry outbursts), unreliable, or erratically present; because they will die imminently; or because they will abandon the patient in favor of someone better.

2. *Mistrust/Abuse.* The expectation that others will hurt, abuse, humiliate, cheat, lie, manipulate, or take advantage. Usually involves the perception that the harm is intentional or the result of unjustified and extreme negligence. May include the sense that one always ends up being cheated relative to others or "getting the short end of the stick."

3. *Emotional Deprivation.* Expectation that one's desire for a normal degree of emotional support will not be adequately met by others. The three major forms of deprivation are:

   (a) *Deprivation of Nurturance* - Absence of attention, affection, warmth, or companionship.
   (b) *Deprivation of Empathy* - Absence of understanding, listening, self-disclosure, or mutual sharing of feelings from others.

(c) *Deprivation of Protection* - Absence of strength, direction, or guidance from others.

4. *Defectiveness/Shame.* The feeling that one is defective, bad, unwanted, inferior, or invalid in important respects; or that one would be unlovable to significant others if exposed. May involve hypersensitivity to criticism, rejection, and blame; self-consciousness, comparisons, and insecurity around others; or a sense of shame regarding one's perceived flaws. These flaws may be *internal* (e.g., selfishness, angry impulses, unacceptable sexual desires) or *external* (e.g., undesirable physical appearance, social awkwardness).

5. *Social Isolation/Alienation.* The feeling that one is isolated from the rest of the world, different from other people, and/or not part of any group or community.

IMPAIRED AUTONOMY AND PERFORMANCE

(Expectations about oneself and the environment that interfere with one's perceived ability to separate, survive, function independently, or perform successfully. Typical family origin is enmeshed, undermining of child's confidence, overprotective, or failing to reinforce child for performing competently outside the family.)

6. *Dependence/Incompetence.* Belief that one is unable to handle one's *everyday responsibilities* in a competent manner, without considerable help from others (e.g., take care of oneself, solve daily problems, exercise good judgment, tackle new tasks, make good decisions). Often presents as helplessness.

7. *Vulnerability to Danger.* Exaggerated fear that "random" catastrophe could strike at any time and that one will be unable to prevent it. Fears focus on one or more of the following: (a) *Medical* - heart attack, AIDS; (b) *Emotional* - go crazy; (c) *Natural/Phobic* - elevators, crime, airplanes, earthquakes.

8. *Enmeshment/Undeveloped Self.* Excessive emotional involvement and closeness with one or more significant others (often parents), at the expense of full individuation or normal social development. Often involves the belief that at least one of the enmeshed individuals cannot survive or be happy without the constant support

of the other. May also include feelings of being smothered by, or fused with, others *or* insufficient individual identity. Often experienced as a feeling of emptiness and floundering, having no direction, or in extreme cases questioning one's existence.

9. *Failure.* The belief that one has failed, will inevitably fail, or is fundamentally inadequate relative to one's peers, in areas of *achievement* (school, career, sports, etc.). Often involves beliefs that one is stupid, inept, untalented, ignorant, lower in status, less successful than others, and so on.

IMPAIRED LIMITS

(Deficiency in internal limits, responsibility to others, or long-term goal-orientation. Leads to difficulty respecting the rights of others, making commitments, or setting and meeting personal goals. Typical family origin is characterized by permissiveness, indulgence, or lack of direction, rather than appropriate confrontation, discipline, and limits in relation to taking responsibility and setting goals. Child may not have been pushed to tolerate normal levels of discomfort, or may not have been given adequate supervision, direction, or guidance.)

10. *Entitlement/Domination.* Insistence that one should be able to do or have whatever one wants, regardless of what others consider reasonable or the cost to others; *or* the excessive tendency to assert one's power, force one's point of view, or control the behavior of others in line with one's own desires - without regard to others' needs for autonomy and self-direction. Often involves excessive demandingness and lack of empathy for others' needs and feelings.

11. *Insufficient Self-Control/Self-Discipline.* Pervasive difficulty or refusal to exercise sufficient self-control and frustration tolerance to achieve one's personal goals, or to restrain the excessive expression of one's emotions and impulses. In its milder form, patient presents with an exaggerated emphasis on *discomfort-avoidance*: avoiding pain, conflict, confrontation, responsibility, or overexertion - at the expense of personal fulfillment, commitment, or integrity.

OTHER-DIRECTEDNESS

(An excessive focus on the desires, feelings, and responses of others, at the expense of one's own needs - in order to gain love and approval, maintain one's sense of

connection, or avoid retaliation. Usually involves suppression and lack of awareness regarding one's own anger and natural inclinations. Typical family origin is based on conditional acceptance: children must suppress important aspects of themselves in order to gain love, attention, and approval. In many such families, the parents' emotional needs and desires - or social acceptance and status - are valued more than the unique needs and feelings of each child.)

12. *Subjugation.* Excessive surrendering of control over one's behavior, emotional expression, and decisions, because one feels *coerced* - usually to avoid anger, retaliation, or abandonment. Involves the perception that one's own desires, opinions, and feelings are not valid or important to others. Frequently presents as excessive compliance, combined with hypersensitivity to feeling trapped.

    Almost always involves the chronic *suppression of anger* toward those perceived to be in control. Usually leads to a build-up of anger that is manifested in maladaptive symptoms (e.g., passive-aggressive behavior, uncontrolled outbursts of temper, psychosomatic symptoms, withdrawal of affection, "acting out," substance abuse).

13. *Self-Sacrifice.* Excessive focus on *voluntarily* meeting the needs of others in daily situations, at the expense of one's own gratification. The most common reasons are to prevent causing pain to others, to avoid guilt from feeling selfish, or to maintain the connection with others perceived as needy. Often results from an acute sensitivity to the pain of others. Sometimes leads to a sense that one's own needs are not being adequately met and to resentment of those who are taken care of. (Overlaps with concept of co-dependency.)

14. *Approval-Seeking.* Excessive emphasis on gaining approval, recognition, or attention from other people, or fitting in, at the expense of developing a secure and true sense of self. One's sense of esteem is dependent primarily on the reactions of others, rather than one's own internalized values, standards, or natural inclinations. Sometimes includes an overemphasis on status, appearance, social acceptance, money, competition, or achievement - being among the best or most popular - as means of gaining approval. Frequently results in major life decisions that are inauthentic or unsatisfying, hypersensitivity to rejection, or envy of others who are more popular or successful.

OVERVIGILANCE AND INHIBITION

(Excessive emphasis on controlling one's spontaneous feelings, impulses, and choices in order to avoid making mistakes or on meeting rigid, internalized rules and expectations about performance and ethical behavior - often at the expense of happiness, self-expression, relaxation, close relationships, or health. Typical family origin is grim [and sometimes punitive]:   performance, duty, perfectionism, following rules, and avoiding costly mistakes predominate over pleasure, joy, and relaxation. There is usually an undercurrent of pessimism and worry - that things could fall apart if one fails to be vigilant and careful at all times.)

15. *Vulnerability to Error/Negativity.* Exaggerated expectation - in a wide range of work, financial, or interpersonal situations that are typically viewed as "controllable" - that things will go seriously wrong, or that aspects of one's life that seem to be going well will fall apart at any time *or* a pervasive, lifelong focus on the negative aspects of life (pain, death, loss, disappointment, conflict, guilt, resentment, unsolved problems, potential mistakes, betrayal, things that could go wrong, etc.) while minimizing or neglecting the positive or optimistic aspects. Usually involves an inordinate fear of making mistakes that might lead to financial collapse, loss, humiliation, being trapped in a bad situation, or loss of control. Because potential negative outcomes are exaggerated, these patients are frequently characterized by chronic worry, vigilance, pessimism, complaining, or indecision.

16. *Overcontrol.*   The excessive inhibition of spontaneous action, feeling, or communication - usually to avoid making mistakes, disapproval by others, catastrophe and chaos, or losing control of one's impulses.   The most common areas of excessive control involve (a) inhibition of *anger* and aggression, (b) compulsive *order* and planning, (c) inhibition of *positive impulses* (e.g., joy, affection, sexual excitement, play), (d) excessive adherence to routine or ritual, and (e) difficulty expressing *vulnerability* or *communicating* freely about one's feelings, needs, and so forth. Often the overcontrol is extended to others in the patient's environment.

17. *Unrelenting Standards.* The underlying belief that one must strive to meet very high *internalized standards* of behavior and performance, usually to avoid criticism.   Typically results in feelings of pressure or difficulty slowing down, and in hypercriticalness toward oneself and others.   Must involve significant impairment in pleasure, relaxation, health, self-esteem, sense of accomplishment, or satisfying relationships.

61

Unrelenting standards typically present as (a) *perfectionism*, inordinate attention to detail, and an underestimate of how good one's own performance is relative to the norm; (b) *rigid rules* or "shoulds" in many areas of life, including unrealistically high moral, ethical, cultural, or religious precepts; or (c) preoccupation with *time and efficiency*, so that more can be accomplished.

18. *Punitiveness.* The tendency to be angry, intolerant, harshly critical, punitive, and impatient with those people (including oneself) who do not meet one's expectations or standards. Usually includes difficulty forgiving mistakes or tolerating limitations in oneself or others, because of a reluctance to consider extenuating circumstances, allow for human imperfection, empathize with feelings, be flexible, or see alternative points of view.

APPENDIX C:
SCHEMA QUESTIONNAIRE
(Second Edition)*

Name_____   Date_____

INSTRUCTIONS

Listed below are statements that a person might use to describe himself or herself. Please read each statement and decide how well it describes you. When you are not sure, base your answer on what you emotionally *feel*, not on what you *think* to be true.

If you desire, reword the statement so that the statement would be even more true of you. Then choose the *highest rating from 1 to 6* that describes you (including your revisions), and write the number in the space before the statement.

RATING SCALE

1 = Completely untrue of me
2 = Mostly untrue of me
3 = Slightly more true than untrue
4 = Moderately true of me
5 = Mostly true of me
6 = Describes me perfectly

EXAMPLE

                              I care about
A. __4__   I worry that people ^ will not like me.

1. _____   People have not been there to meet my emotional needs.

---

*Developed by Jeffrey E. Young, PhD, and Gary Brown, MEd. Copyright © 1990 by the authors. Unauthorized reproduction without written consent of the authors is prohibited. For more information, write: Cognitive Therapy Center of New York, 3 East 80th Street - Penthouse, New York, NY 10021 or telephone (212) 717-1052.

2. _____ I haven't gotten love and attention.

3. _____ For the most part, I haven't had someone to depend on for advice and emotional support.

4. _____ Most of the time, I haven't had someone to nurture me, share himself/herself with me, or care deeply about everything that happens to me.

5. _____ For much of my life, I haven't had someone who wanted to get close to me and spend a lot of time with me.

6. _____ In general, people have not been there to give me warmth, holding, and affection.

7. _____ For much of my life, I haven't felt that I am special to someone.

8. _____ For the most part, I have not had someone who really listens to me, understands me, or is tuned into my true needs and feelings.

9. _____ I have rarely had a strong person to give me sound advice or direction when I'm not sure what to do.

*ed

10. _____ I worry that the people I love will die soon, even though there is little medical reason to support my concern.

11. _____ I find myself clinging to people I'm close to because I'm afraid they'll leave me.

12. _____ I worry that people I feel close to will leave me or abandon me.

13. _____ I feel that I lack a stable base of emotional support.

14. _____ I don't feel that important relationships will last; I expect them to end.

15. _____ I feel addicted to partners who can't be there for me in a committed way.

16. _____ In the end, I will be alone.

17. _____ When I feel someone I care for pulling away from me, I get desperate.

18. _____ Sometimes I am so worried about people leaving me that I drive them away.

19. _____ I become upset when someone leaves me alone, even for a short period of time.

20. _____ I can't count on people who support me to be there on a regular basis.

21. _____ I can't let myself get really close to other people because I can't be sure they'll always be there.

22. _____ It seems that the important people in my life are always coming and going.

23. _____ I worry a lot that the people I love will find someone else they prefer and leave me.

24. _____ The people close to me have been very unpredictable; one moment they're available and nice to me; the next, they're angry, upset, self-absorbed, fighting, and so on.

25. _____ I need other people so much that I worry about losing them.

26. _____ I feel so defenseless if I don't have people to protect me that I worry a lot about losing them.

27. _____ I can't be myself or express what I really feel, or people will leave me.

   *ab

28. _____ I feel that people will take advantage of me.

29. _____ I often feel that I have to protect myself from other people.

30. _____ I feel that I cannot let my guard down in the presence of other people, or else they will intentionally hurt me.

31. _____ If someone acts nicely towards me, I assume that he/she must be after something.

32. _____ It is only a matter of time before someone betrays me.

33. _____ Most people only think about themselves.

34. _____ I have a great deal of difficulty trusting people.

35. _____ I am quite suspicious of other people's motives.

36. _____ Other people are rarely honest; they are usually not what they appear.

37. _____ I'm usually on the lookout for people's ulterior motives.

38. _____ If I think someone is out to hurt me, I try to hurt them first.

39. _____ People usually have to prove themselves to me before I can trust them.

40. _____ I set up "tests" for other people to see if they are telling me the truth and are well-intentioned.

41. _____ I subscribe to the belief: "Control or be controlled."

42. _____ I get angry when I think about the ways I have been mistreated by other people throughout my life.

43. _____ Throughout my life, those close to me have taken advantage of me or used me for their own purposes.

44. _____ I have been physically, emotionally, or sexually abused by important people in my life.
    *ma

45. _____ I don't fit in.

46. _____ I'm fundamentally different from other people.

47. _____ I don't belong; I'm a loner.

48. _____ I feel alienated from other people.

49. _____ I feel isolated and alone.

50. _____ I always feel on the outside of groups.

51. _____ No one really understands me.

52. _____ My family was always different from the families around us.

53. _____ I sometimes feel as if I'm an alien.

54. _____ If I disappeared tomorrow, no one would notice.
    *si

55. _____ No man/woman I desire could love me once he/she saw my defects.

56. _____ No one I desire would want to stay close to me if he/she knew the real me.

57. _____ I am inherently flawed and defective.

58. _____ No matter how hard I try, I feel that I won't be able to get a significant man/woman to respect me or feel that I am worthwhile.

59. _____ I'm unworthy of the love, attention, and respect of others.

60. _____ I feel that I'm not lovable.

61. _____ I am too unacceptable in very basic ways to reveal myself to other people.

62. _____ If others found out about my basic defects, I could not face them.

63. _____ When people like me, I feel I am fooling them.

64. _____ I often find myself drawn to people who are very critical or reject me.

65. _____ I have inner secrets that I don't want people close to me to find out.

66. _____ It is my fault that my parent(s) could not love me enough.

67. _____ I don't let people know the real me.

68. _____ One of my greatest fears is that my defects will be exposed.

69. _____ I cannot understand how anyone could love me.
    *ds

70. _____ I'm not sexually attractive.

71. _____ I'm too fat.

72. _____ I'm ugly.

73. _____ I can't carry on a decent conversation.

74. _____ I'm dull and boring in social situations.

75. _____ People I value wouldn't associate with me because of my social status (e.g., income, educational level, career).

76. _____ I never know what to say socially.

77. _____ People don't want to include me in their groups.

78. _____ I am very self-conscious around other people.
    *su

79. _____ Almost nothing I do at work (or school) is as good as what other people can do.

80. _____ I'm incompetent when it comes to achievement.

81. _____ Most other people are more capable than I am in areas of work and achievement.

82. _____ I'm a failure.

83. _____ I'm not as talented as most people are at their work.

84. _____ I'm not as intelligent as most people when it comes to work (or school).

85. _____ I am humiliated by my failures and inadequacies in the work sphere.

86. _____ I often feel embarrassed around other people because I don't measure up to them in terms of my accomplishments.

87. _____ I often compare my accomplishments with others and feel that they are much more successful.

    *fa

88. _____ I do not feel capable of getting by on my own in everyday life.

89. _____ I need other people to help me get by.

90. _____ I do not feel I can cope well by myself.

91. _____ I believe that other people can take care of me better than I can take care of myself.

92. _____ I have trouble tackling new tasks outside of work unless I have someone to guide me.

93. _____ I think of myself as a dependent person, when it comes to everyday functioning.

94. _____ I screw up everything I try, even outside of work (or school).

95. _____ I'm inept in most areas of life.

96. _____ If I trust my own judgment in everyday situations, I'll make the wrong decision.

97. _____ I lack common sense.

98. _____ My judgment cannot be relied upon in everyday situations.

99. _____ I don't feel confident about my ability to solve everyday problems that come up.

100. _____ I feel I need someone I can rely on to give me advice about practical issues.

101. _____ I feel more like a child than an adult when it comes to handling everyday responsibilities.

102. _____ I find the responsibilities of everyday life overwhelming.
    *di

103. _____ I can't seem to escape the feeling that something bad is about to happen.

104. _____ I feel that a disaster (natural, criminal, financial, or medical) could strike at any moment.

105. _____ I worry about becoming a street person or vagrant.

106. _____ I worry about being attacked.

107. _____ I feel that I must be very careful about money or else I might end up with nothing.

108. _____ I take great precautions to avoid getting sick or hurt.

109. _____ I worry that I'll lose all my money and become destitute.

110. _____ I worry that I'm developing a serious illness, even though nothing serious has been diagnosed by a physician.

111. _____ I am a fearful person.

112. _____ I worry a lot about the bad things happening in the world: crime, pollution, and so on.

113. _____ I often feel that I might go crazy.

114. _____ I often feel that I'm going to have an anxiety attack.

115. _____ I often worry that I might have a heart attack, even though there is little medical reason to be concerned.

116. _____ I feel that the world is a dangerous place.
 *vh

117. _____ I have not been able to separate myself from my parent(s), the way other people my age seem to.

118. _____ My parent(s) and I tend to be overinvolved in each other's lives and problems.

119. _____ It is very difficult for my parent(s) and me to keep intimate details from each other, without feeling betrayed or guilty.

120. _____ My parent(s) and I have to speak to each other almost every day or else one of us feels guilty, hurt, disappointed, or alone.

121. _____ I often feel that I do not have a separate identity from my parents or partner.

122. _____ I often feel as if my parents are living through me - I don't have a life of my own.

123. _____ It is very difficult for me to maintain any distance from the people I am intimate with; I have trouble keeping any separate sense of myself.

124. _____ I am so involved with my partner or parents that I do not really know who I am or what I want.

125. _____ I have trouble separating my point of view or opinion from that of my parents or partner.

126. _____ I often feel that I have no privacy when it comes to my parents or partner.

127. _____ I feel that my parents are, or would be, very hurt about my living on my own, away from them.
 *em

128. _____ I let other people have their way because I fear the consequences.

129. _____ I think if I do what I want, I'm only asking for trouble.

130. _____ I feel that I have no choice but to give in to other peoples' wishes, or else they will retaliate or reject me in some way.

131. _____ In relationships, I let the other person have the upper hand.

132. _____ I've always let others make choices for me, so I really don't know what I want for myself.

133. _____ I feel the major decisions in my life were not really my own.

134. _____ I worry a lot about pleasing other people so they won't reject me.

135. _____ I have a lot of trouble demanding that my rights be respected and that my feelings be taken into account.

136. _____ I get back at people in little ways instead of showing my anger.

137. _____ I will go to much greater lengths than most people to avoid confrontations.
     *sb

138. _____ I put others' needs before my own or else I feel guilty.

139. _____ I feel guilty when I let other people down or disappoint them.

140. _____ I give more to other people than I get back in return.

141. _____ I'm the one who usually ends up taking care of the people I'm close to.

142. _____ There is almost nothing I couldn't put up with if I loved someone.

143. _____ I am a good person because I think of others more than of myself.

144. _____ At work, I'm usually the one to volunteer to do extra tasks or to put in extra time.

145. _____ No matter how busy I am, I can always find time for others.

146. _____ I can get by on very little because my needs are minimal.

147. _____ I'm only happy when those around me are happy.

148. _____ I'm so busy doing for the people that I care about that I have little time for myself.

149. _____ I've always been the one who listens to everyone else's problems.

150. _____ I'm more comfortable giving a present than receiving one.

151. _____ Other people see me as doing too much for others and not enough for myself.

152. _____ No matter how much I give, it is never enough.

153. _____ If I do what I want, I feel very uncomfortable.

154. _____ It's very difficult for me to ask others to take care of my needs.

*ss

155. _____ I worry about losing control of my actions.

156. _____ I worry that I might seriously harm someone physically or emotionally if my anger gets out of control.

157. _____ I feel that I must control my emotions and impulses or something bad is likely to happen.

158. _____ A lot of anger and resentment build up inside of me that I don't express.

159. _____ I am too self-conscious to show positive feelings to others (e.g., affection, showing I care).

160. _____ I find it embarrassing to express my feelings to others.

161. _____ I find it hard to be warm and spontaneous.

162. _____ I control myself so much that people think I am unemotional.

163. _____ People see me as uptight emotionally.
 *ei

164. _____ I must be the best at most of what I do; I can't accept second best.

165. _____ I strive to keep almost everything in perfect order.

166. _____ I must look my best most of the time.

167. _____ I try to do my best; I can't settle for "good enough."

168. _____ I have so much to accomplish that there is almost no time to really relax.

169. _____ Almost nothing I do is quite good enough; I can always do better.

170. _____ I must meet all my responsibilities.

171. _____ I feel there is constant pressure for me to achieve and get things done.

172. _____ My relationships suffer because I push myself so hard.

173. _____ My health is suffering because I put myself under so much pressure to do well.

174. _____ I often sacrifice pleasure and happiness to meet my own standards.

175. _____ When I make a mistake, I deserve strong criticism.

176. _____ I can't let myself off the hook easily or make excuses for my mistakes.

177. _____ I'm a very competitive person.

178. _____ I put a good deal of emphasis on money or status.

179. _____ I always have to be "Number One," in terms of my performance.
*us

180. _____ I have a lot of trouble accepting "no" for an answer when I want something from other people.

181. _____ I often get angry or irritable if I can't get what I want.

182. _____ I'm special and shouldn't have to accept many of the restrictions placed on other people.

183. _____ I hate to be constrained or kept from doing what I want.

184. _____ I feel that I shouldn't have to follow the normal rules and conventions other people do.

185. _____ I feel that what I have to offer is of greater value than the contributions of others.

186. _____ I usually put my needs ahead of the needs of others.

187. _____ I often find that I am so involved in my own priorities that I don't have time to give to friends or family.

188. _____ People often tell me I am very controlling about the ways things are done.

189. _____ I get very irritated when people won't do what I ask of them.

190. _____ I can't tolerate other people telling me what to do.
*et

191. _____ I have great difficulty getting myself to stop drinking, smoking, overeating, or other problem behaviors.

192. _____ I can't seem to discipline myself to complete routine or boring tasks.

193. _____ Often I allow myself to carry through on impulses and express emotions that get me into trouble or hurt other people.

194. _____ If I can't reach a goal, I become easily frustrated and give up.

195. _____ I have a very difficult time sacrificing immediate gratification to achieve a long-range goal.

196. _____ It often happens that, once I start to feel angry, I just can't control it.

197. _____ I tend to overdo things, even though I know they are bad for me.

198. _____ I get bored very easily.

199. _____ When tasks become difficult, I usually cannot persevere and complete them.

200. _____ I can't concentrate on anything for too long.

201. _____ I can't force myself to do things I don't enjoy, even when I know it's for my own good.

202. _____ I lose my temper at the slightest offense.

203. _____ I have rarely been able to stick to my resolutions.

204. _____ I can almost never hold back from showing people how I really feel, no matter what the cost may be.

205. _____ I often do things impulsively that I later regret.

*is

Interpreting the
SCHEMA QUESTIONNAIRE (2nd ed.)

We do not yet have statistical norms for the *Schema Questionnaire*, although this research is in progress. In the meantime, we have developed the following informal procedures for clinical use.

Items on the questionnaire are clustered according to specific schemas. These clusters of items are separated by an asterisk and a two letter code that is an abbreviation for the schema. For example, Items 1-9 are followed by the abbreviation "*ed," indicating that these specific items assess the Emotional Deprivation schema. The abbreviations for the 16 schemas are:

ed - Emotional Deprivation
ab - Abandonment
ma - Mistrust/Abuse
si - Social Isolation
ds - Defectiveness/Shame
su - Social Undesirability
fa - Failure to Achieve
di - Functional Dependence/Incompetence
vh - Vulnerability to Harm and Illness
em - Enmeshment
sb - Subjugation
ss - Self-Sacrifice
ei - Emotional Inhibition
us - Unrelenting Standards
et - Entitlement
is - Insufficient Self-Control/Self-Discipline

APPENDIX D: A CLIENT'S GUIDE TO SCHEMA-FOCUSED COGNITIVE THERAPY*

HARRY is a 45-year-old middle-level manager. He has been married for 16 years, but his marriage has been very troubled. He and his wife are often resentful of each other, they rarely communicate on an intimate level, and they have few moments of real pleasure.

Other aspects of Harry's life have been equally unsatisfying. He doesn't enjoy his work, primarily because he doesn't get along with his co-workers. He is often intimidated by his boss and other people at the office. He has a few friends outside of work, but none that he considers close.

During the past year Harry's mood became increasingly negative. He was getting more irritable, he had trouble sleeping, and he began to have difficulty concentrating at work. As he became more and more depressed, he began to eat more and gained 15 pounds. When he found himself thinking about taking his own life, he decided it was time to get help. He consulted a psychologist who practices cognitive therapy.

As a result of short-term cognitive therapy techniques, Harry improved rapidly. His mood lifted, his appetite returned to normal, and he no longer thought about suicide. In addition he was able to concentrate well again and was much less irritable. He also began to feel more in control of his life as he learned how to control his emotions for the first time.

But, in some ways, the short-term techniques were not enough. His relationships with his wife and others, while they no longer depressed him as much as they had, still failed to give him much pleasure. He still could not ask to have his needs met, and he had few experiences he considered truly enjoyable. The therapist then began schema-focused cognitive therapy to help Harry change his long-term life patterns.

This guide will present the *schema-focused* approach, a recent elaboration of cognitive therapy developed by Dr. Jeffrey Young that can help people change long-term patterns, including the ways in which they interact with other people. This overview of schema-focused cognitive therapy consists of five parts:

---

*Developed by David C. Bricker, PhD, and Jeffrey E. Young, PhD. Copyright © 1993 by Cognitive Therapy Center of New York. Unauthorized reproduction without written consent of the authors is prohibited. For more information, write: Cognitive Therapy Center of New York, 3 East 80th Street - Penthouse, New York, NY 10021 or telephone (212) 717-1052.

1. A brief presentation of short-term cognitive therapy.
2. An explanation of what a schema is and examples of schemas.
3. An explanation of the processes by which schemas function.
4. Several case examples.
5. A brief description of the therapeutic process.

SHORT-TERM COGNITIVE THERAPY

Cognitive therapy is a system of psychotherapy developed by Aaron Beck and his colleagues to help people overcome emotional problems. This system emphasizes changing the ways in which people think in order to improve their moods, such as depression, anxiety, and anger.

Emotional disturbance is influenced by the cognitive distortions that people make in dealing with their life experiences. These distortions take the form of negative interpretations and predictions of everyday events. For instance, a male college student preparing for a test might make himself feel discouraged by thinking: *"This material is impossible"* (Negative Interpretation) and *"I'll never pass this test"* (Negative Prediction).

The therapy consists of helping clients to restructure their thinking. An important step in this process is examining the evidence concerning the maladaptive thoughts. In the example above, the therapist would help the student to look at his past experiences and determine if the material was in fact impossible to learn, and if he knew for sure that he couldn't pass the test. In all probability, the student would decide that these two thoughts lacked validity.

More accurate alternative thoughts would be substituted. For instance, the student might be encouraged to think: *"This material is difficult, but not impossible. I've learned difficult material before"* and *"I've never failed a test before, so long as I've done enough preparation."* These thoughts would probably lead him to feel better and cope better.

Often short-term cognitive therapy is enough to help people overcome emotional problems, especially depression and anxiety. Recent research has shown this to be so. However, sometimes this approach is not enough. Some clients in short-term cognitive therapy find that they don't get all the benefits they want. This has led us to develop *schema-focused cognitive therapy*.

SCHEMAS - WHAT THEY ARE

A schema is an extremely stable and enduring pattern that develops during childhood and is elaborated throughout an individual's life. We view the world through our schemas.

Schemas are important beliefs and feelings about oneself and the environment which the individual accepts without question. They are self-perpetuating, and are very resistant to change. For instance, children who develop a schema that they are incompetent rarely challenge this belief, even as adults. The schema usually does not go away without therapy. Overwhelming success in people's lives is often still not enough to change the schema. The schema fights for its own survival, and, usually, is quite successful.

Even though schemas persist once they are formed, they are not always in our awareness. Usually they operate in subtle ways, out of our awareness. However, when a schema erupts or is triggered by events, our thoughts and feelings are dominated by these schemas. It is at these moments that people tend to experience extreme negative emotions and have dysfunctional thoughts.

In our work with many patients, we have found 16 specific schemas. Most clients have at least two or three of these schemas, and often more. A brief description of each of these schemas is provided below.

Emotional Deprivation

This schema refers to the belief that one's primary emotional needs will never be met by others. These needs include nurturance, empathy, affection, protection, guidance, and caring from others. Often parents were emotionally depriving to the child.

Abandonment/Instability

This schema refers to the expectation that one will soon lose anyone with whom an emotional attachment is formed. The person believes that, one way or another, close relationships will end imminently. As children, these clients may have experienced the divorce or death of parents. This schema can also arise when parents have been inconsistent in attending to the child's needs; for instance, there may have been frequent occasions on which the child was left alone or unattended to for extended periods.

Mistrust/Abuse

This schema refers to the expectation that others will intentionally take advantage in some way. People with this schema expect others to hurt, cheat, or put them down. They often think in terms of attacking first or getting revenge afterwards. In childhood, these clients were often abused or treated unfairly by parents, siblings, or peers.

Social Isolation/Alienation

This schema refers to the belief that one is isolated from the world, different from other people, and/or not part of any community. This belief is usually caused by early experiences in which children see that either they, or their families, are different from other people.

Defectiveness/Shame

This schema refers to the belief that one is *internally* flawed, and that, if others get close, they will realize this and withdraw from the relationship. This feeling of being flawed and inadequate often leads to a strong sense of shame. Generally parents were very critical of their children and made them feel as if they were not worthy of being loved.

Social Undesirability

This schema refers to the belief that one is *outwardly* unattractive to others. People with this schema see themselves as physically unattractive, socially inept, or lacking in status. Usually there is a direct link to childhood experiences in which children are made to feel, by family or peers, that they are not attractive.

Failure to Achieve

This schema refers to the belief that one is incapable of performing as well as one's peers in areas such as career, school, or sports. These clients may feel stupid, inept, untalented, or ignorant. People with this schema often do not try to achieve because they believe that they will fail. This schema may develop if children are put down and treated as if they are a failure in school or other spheres of accomplishment. Usually the parents did not give enough support, discipline, and encouragement for the child to persist and succeed in areas of achievement such as schoolwork or sports.

Functional Dependence/Incompetence

This schema refers to the belief that one is not capable of handling day-to-day responsibilities competently and independently. People with this schema often rely on others excessively for help in areas such as decision making and initiating new tasks. Generally, parents did not encourage these children to act independently and develop confidence in their ability to take care of themselves.

Vulnerability to Harm and Illness

This schema refers to the belief that one is always on the verge of experiencing a major catastrophe (financial, natural, medical, criminal, etc.). It may lead to taking excessive precautions to protect oneself. Usually there was an extremely fearful parent who passed on the idea that the world is a dangerous place.

Undeveloped Self

This schema refers to the sense that one has too little individual identity or inner direction. There is often a feeling of emptiness or of floundering. This schema is often brought on by parents who are so controlling, abusive, or overprotective that the child is discouraged from developing a separate sense of self.

Subjugation

This schema refers to the belief that one must submit to the control of others in order to avoid negative consequences. Often these clients fear that, unless they submit, others will get angry or reject them. Clients who subjugate ignore their own desires and feelings. In childhood there was generally a very controlling parent.

Self-Sacrifice

This schema refers to the excessive sacrifice of one's own needs in order to help others. When these clients pay attention to their own needs, they often feel guilty. To avoid this guilt, they put others' needs ahead of their own. Often clients who self-sacrifice gain a feeling of increased self-esteem or a sense of meaning from helping others. In childhood the person may have been made to feel overly responsible for the well-being of one or both parents.

Emotional Inhibition

This schema refers to the belief that you must inhibit emotions and impulses, especially *anger*, because any expression of feelings would harm others or lead to loss of self-esteem, embarrassment, retaliation, or abandonment. You may lack spontaneity, or be viewed as uptight. This schema is often brought on by parents who discourage the expression of feelings.

Unrelenting/Unbalanced Standards

This schema refers to two related beliefs. Either you believe that whatever you do is not good enough, that you must always strive harder; and/or there is excessive emphasis on values such as status, wealth, and power at the expense of other values such as social interaction, health, or happiness. Usually these clients' parents were never satisfied and gave their children love that was conditional on outstanding achievement.

Entitlement/Self-Centeredness

This schema refers to the belief that you should be able to do, say, or have whatever you want immediately regardless of whether that hurts others or seems reasonable to them. You are not interested in what other people need, nor are you aware of the long-term costs to you of alienating others. Parents who overindulge their children and who do not set limits about what is socially appropriate may foster the development of this schema. Alternatively, some children develop this schema to compensate for feelings of emotional deprivation, defectiveness, or social undesirability.

Insufficient Self-Control/Self-Discipline

This schema refers to the inability to tolerate any frustration in reaching one's goals, as well as an inability to restrain expression of one's impulses or feelings. When lack of self-control is extreme, criminal or addictive behavior rule your life. Parents who did not model self-control, or who did not adequately discipline their children, may predispose them to have this schema as adults.

HOW SCHEMAS WORK

In order to understand how schemas work, there are three schema processes that must be defined. These processes are *schema maintenance, schema avoidance,* and *schema compensation.* It is through these three processes that schemas exert their influence on our behavior and work to insure their own survival.

Schema Maintenance

Schema maintenance refers to the routine processes by which schemas function and perpetuate themselves. This is accomplished by cognitive distortions and self-defeating behavior patterns.

Earlier we mentioned that cognitive distortions are a central part of cognitive therapy. These distortions consist of negative interpretations and predictions of life events. Many cognitive distortions are part of the schema maintenance process. The schema will highlight or exaggerate information that confirms the schema and will minimize or deny information that contradicts it.

Schema maintenance works behaviorally as well as cognitively. The schema will generate behaviors which tend to keep the schema intact. For instance, a young man with a **Social Undesirability** schema would have thoughts and behaviors in line with the schema. At a party he would have thoughts such as: *"No one here likes me"* and *"I'm not going to succeed at meeting new people."* Behaviorally, he would be more withdrawn and less outgoing.

Schema Avoidance

Schema avoidance refers to the ways in which people avoid activating schemas. As mentioned earlier, when schemas are activated, this causes extreme negative emotion. People develop ways to avoid triggering schemas in order not to feel this pain. There are three types of schema avoidance: *cognitive, emotional,* and *behavioral.*

Cognitive avoidance refers to efforts that people make not to think about upsetting events. These efforts may be either voluntary or automatic. People may voluntarily choose not to focus on an aspect of their personality or an event which they find disturbing. There are also unconscious processes which help people to shut out information which would be too upsetting to confront. People often forget particularly painful events. For instance, children who have been abused sexually often forget the memory completely.

Emotional or affective avoidance refers to automatic or voluntary attempts to block painful emotion. Often when people have painful emotional experiences, they numb themselves to the feelings in order to minimize the pain. For instance, a man might talk about how his wife has been acting in an abusive manner toward him and say that he feels no anger towards her, only a little annoyance. Some people drink or abuse drugs to numb feelings generated by schemas.

The third type of avoidance is *behavioral* avoidance. People often act in such a way as to avoid situations that trigger schemas, and thus avoid psychological pain. For instance, a woman with a **Failure to Achieve** schema might avoid taking a difficult new job which would be very good for her. By avoiding the challenging situation, she avoids any pain, such as intense anxiety, which could be generated by the schema.

Schema Compensation

The third schema process is schema compensation. The individual behaves in a manner which appears to be the opposite of what the schema suggests in order to avoid triggering the schema. People with a **Functional Dependence** schema may structure aspects of their life so that they don't have to depend on anyone, even when a more balanced approach may be better. For instance, a young man may refuse to go out with women because he is afraid of becoming dependent and will present himself as someone who doesn't need other people. He goes to the other extreme to avoid feeling dependent.

CASE EXAMPLES

In this section six case examples are presented. In each one, the schema processes are demonstrated. By reading through this section, you will get a better feel for how these processes can operate in real life situations.

Abby is a young woman whose main schema is **Subjugation**. She tends to see people as very controlling even when they are being appropriately assertive. She has thoughts such as *"I can't stand up for myself or they won't like me"* and is likely to give in to others (**Schema Maintenance**). At other times she decides that no one will get the better of her and becomes very controlling (**Schema Compensation**). Sometimes when people make unreasonable demands on her she minimizes the importance of her own feelings and has thoughts like *"It's not that important to me what happens."* At other times she avoids acquaintances with whom she has trouble standing up for herself (**Schema Avoidance**).

Stewart's main schema is **Failure to Achieve**. Whenever he is faced with a possible challenge, he tends to think that he is not capable. Often he tries half-heartedly, guaranteeing that he will fail, and strengthening the belief that he is not capable (**Schema Maintenance**). At times, he makes great efforts to present himself in an unrealistically positive light by spending excessive amounts of money on items such as clothing and automobiles (**Schema Compensation**). Often he avoids triggering his schema by staying away from challenges altogether and convinces himself that the challenge was not worth taking (**Schema Avoidance**).

Rebecca's core schema is **Defectiveness/Shame**. She believes that there is something basically wrong with her and that if anyone gets too close, the person will reject her. She chooses partners who are extremely critical of her and confirm her view that she is defective (**Schema Maintenance**).

Sometimes she has an excessive defensive reaction and counterattacks when confronted with even mild criticism (**Schema Compensation**). She also makes sure that none of her partners get too close, so that she can avoid their seeing her defectiveness and rejecting her (**Schema Avoidance**).

Michael is a middle-aged man whose main schema is **Functional Dependence/Incompetence**. He sees himself as being incapable of doing daily tasks on his own and generally seeks the support of others. Whenever he can, he chooses to work with people who help him out to an excessive degree. This keeps him from developing skills needed to work alone and confirms his view of himself as someone who needs others to help him out (**Schema Maintenance**). At times, when he would be best off taking advice from other people, he refuses to do so (**Schema Compensation**). He reduces his anxiety by procrastinating as much as he can get away with (**Schema Avoidance**).

Ann's core schema is **Social Isolation**. She sees herself as being different from other people and not fitting in. When she does things as part of a group she does not get really involved (**Schema Maintenance**). At times she gets very hostile towards group members and can be very critical of the group as a whole (**Schema Compensation**). At other times she chooses to avoid group activities altogether (**Schema Avoidance**).

Sam's central schema is **Emotional Deprivation**. He chooses partners who are not very capable of giving to other people and then acts in a manner which makes it even more difficult for them to give to him (**Schema Maintenance**). At times he will act in a very demanding, belligerent manner and provoke fights with his partners (**Schema Compensation**). Sam avoids getting too close to women, yet denies that he has any problems in this area (**Schema Avoidance**).

THERAPEUTIC PROCESS - CHANGING SCHEMAS

In schema-focused cognitive therapy the goal of the treatment is to weaken the early maladaptive schemas as much as possible and build up the person's healthy side. An alliance is formed between the therapist and the healthy part of the client against the schemas.

The first step in therapy is to do a comprehensive assessment of the client. The main goal of this assessment is to identify the schemas that are most important in the client's psychological makeup. There are several steps to this process. The therapist generally will first want to know about recent events or circumstances in the clients' lives that have led them to come for help. The therapist will then discuss the client's life history and look for patterns which may be related to schemas.

There are several other steps the therapist will take in assessing schemas. There is a "Schema Questionnaire" which the client fills out, listing many of the thoughts related to the different schemas; items on this questionnaire can be rated as to how relevant to the client's life they are.

There are also various imagery techniques which the therapist can use to assess schemas. One specific technique involves asking clients to close their eyes and create an image of themselves as children with their families. Often the images that appear will lead to the core schemas.

Jonathan is a 28-year-old executive whose core schema is **Mistrust/Abuse**. He came to therapy because he was having bouts of intense anxiety at work, during which he would be overly suspicious and resentful of his co-workers. When asked to create an image of himself with his family, he had two different images. In the first he saw himself being terrorized by his older brother. In the second he saw his alcoholic father coming home and beating his mother, while he cowered in fear.

There are many techniques which the therapist can use to help clients weaken their schemas. These techniques can be broken down into four categories: *emotive, interpersonal, cognitive,* and *behavioral*. Each of these categories will be briefly discussed, along with a few examples.

Emotive Techniques

Emotive techniques encourage clients to experience and express the emotional aspects of their problem. One way this is done is by having clients close their eyes and imagine they are having a conversation with the person to whom the emotion is directed. They are then encouraged to express the emotions as completely as possible in the imaginary dialogue. One woman whose core schema was **Emotional Deprivation** had several such sessions in which she had an opportunity to express her anger at her parents for not being there enough for her emotionally. Each time she expressed these feelings, she was able to distance herself further from the schema. She was able to see that her parents had their own problems which kept them from providing her with adequate nurturance, and that she was not always destined to be deprived.

There are many variations on the above technique. Clients may take on the role of the other person in these dialogues and express what they imagine their feelings to be. Or they may write a letter to the other person, which they have no intention of mailing, so that they can express their feelings without inhibition.

Interpersonal Techniques

Interpersonal techniques highlight the client's interactions with other people so that the role of the schemas can be exposed. One way is by focusing on the relationship with the therapist. Frequently, clients with a **Subjugation** schema go along with everything the therapist wants, even when they do not consider the assignment or activity relevant. They then feel resentment towards the therapist which they display indirectly. This pattern of compliance and indirect expression of resentment can then be explored to the client's benefit. This may lead to a useful exploration of other instances in which the client complies with others and later resents it, and how the client might better cope at those times.

Another type of interpersonal technique involves including a client's spouse in therapy. A man with a **Self-Sacrifice** schema might choose a wife who tends to ignore his wishes. The therapist may wish to involve the wife in the treatment in order to help the two of them to explore the patterns in their relationship and change the ways in which they interact.

Cognitive Techniques

Cognitive techniques are those in which the schema-driven cognitive distortions are challenged. As in short-term cognitive therapy, the dysfunctional thoughts are identified and the evidence for and against them is considered. Then new thoughts and beliefs are substituted. These techniques help the client see alternative ways to view situations.

The first step in dealing with schemas cognitively is to examine the evidence for and against the specific schema which is being examined. This involves looking at the client's life and experiences and considering all the evidence which appears to support or refute the schema. The evidence is then examined critically to see if it does, in fact, provide support for the schema. Usually the evidence produced will be shown to be in error, and not really supportive of the schema.

For instance, let's consider a young man with an **Emotional Deprivation** schema. When asked for evidence that his emotional needs will never be met, he brings up instances in which past girlfriends have not met his needs. However, when these past relationships are looked at carefully, he finds that, as part of the schema maintenance process, he has chosen women who are not capable of giving emotionally.

This understanding gives him a sense of optimism; if he starts selecting his partners differently, his needs can probably be met.

Another cognitive technique is to have a structured dialogue between the client and therapist. First, the client takes the side of the schema, and the therapist presents a more constructive view. Then the two switch sides, giving the client a chance to verbalize the alternative point of view.

After having several of these dialogues the client and therapist can then construct a flashcard for the client, which contains a concise statement of the evidence against the schema.

A typical flashcard for a client with a **Defectiveness/Shame** schema reads: *"I know that I feel that there is something wrong with me but the healthy side of me knows that I'm OK. There have been several people who have known me very well and stayed with me for a long time. I know that I can pursue friendships with many people in whom I have an interest."*

The client is instructed to keep the flashcard available at all times and to read it whenever the relevant problem starts to occur. By persistent practice at this and other cognitive techniques, the client's belief in the schema will gradually weaken.

Behavioral Techniques

Behavioral techniques are those in which the therapist assists the client in changing long-term behavior patterns, so that schema maintenance behaviors are reduced and healthy coping responses are strengthened.

One behavioral strategy is to help clients choose partners who are appropriate for them and capable of engaging in healthy relationships. Clients with the **Emotional Deprivation** schema tend to choose partners who are not emotionally giving. A therapist working with such clients would help them through the process of evaluating and selecting new patterns.

Another behavioral technique consists of teaching clients better communication skills. For instance, a woman with a **Subjugation** schema believes that she deserves a raise at work but does not know how to ask for it. One technique her therapist uses to teach her how to speak to her supervisor is role playing. First, the therapist takes the role of the client and the client takes the role of the supervisor. This allows the therapist to demonstrate how to make the request appropriately. Then the client gets an opportunity to practice the new behaviors and to get feedback from the therapist before changing the behavior in real-life situations.

IN SUMMARY, schema-focused cognitive therapy can help people understand and change long-term life patterns. The therapy consists of identifying early maladaptive schemas and systematically confronting and challenging them.

REFERENCES

American Psychiatric Association. (1987). *Diagnostic and Statistical Manual of Mental Disorders* (3rd ed. rev.). Washington, DC: Author.

American Psychiatric Association. (1994). *Diagnostic and Statistical Manual of Mental Disorders* (4th ed.). Washington, DC: Author.

Beck, A. T. (1967). *Depression: Causes and Treatment.* Philadelphia: University of Pennsylvania Press.

Beck, A. T., Rush, A. J., Shaw, B. F., & Emery, G. (1979). *Cognitive Therapy of Depression.* New York: Guilford.

Bowlby, J. (1973). *Separation: Anxiety and Anger* (Vol. II of *Attachment and Loss*). New York: Basic Books.

Corr, E. (Director). (1986). *Desert Bloom* [Film].

Guidano, V. F., & Liotti, G. (1983). *Cognitive Processes and Emotional Disorders.* New York: Guilford.

Kaplan, H. I., & Sadock, B. J. (1985). *Comprehensive Textbook of Psychiatry* (4th ed.). Baltimore: Williams & Wilkins.

Lazarus, A., & Lazarus, C. (1991). *Multimodal Life History Inventory* (2nd ed.). Champaign, IL: Research Press.

Miller, A. (1981). *The Drama of the Gifted Child.* (Originally published as *Prisoners of Childhood*). New York: Basic Books.

Millon, T. (1981). *Disorders of Personality.* New York: John Wiley & Sons.

Segal, Z. (1988). Appraisal of the self-schema: Construct in cognitive models of depression. *Psychological Bulletin, 103,* 147-162.

Young, J. E., & Klosko, J. (1993). *Reinventing Your Life.* New York: Dutton (An Imprint of Penguin USA).

If You Found This Book Useful . . .

You might want to know more about our other titles.

If you would like to receive our latest catalog, please return this form:

Name:_____
(Please Print)

Address:_____

Address:_____

City/State/Zip:_____
This is ☐ home   ☐ office

Telephone:(_____)_____

I am a:

_____ Psychologist	_____ Mental Health Counselor
_____ Psychiatrist	_____ Marriage and Family Therapist
_____ School Psychologist	_____ Not in Mental Health Field
_____ Clinical Social Worker	_____ Other:_____

◆   ◆   ◆

Professional Resource Press
P.O. Box 15560
Sarasota, FL 34277-1560

Telephone #800-443-3364

E-mail at mail@prpress.com

CTPD/11/98

Add A Colleague To Our Mailing List . . .

If you would like us to send our latest catalog to one of your colleagues, please return this form.

Name:_____
(Please Print)

Address:_____

Address:_____

City/State/Zip:_____
This is ❑ home ❑ office

Telephone:(_____)_____

This person is a:

_____ Psychologist   _____ Mental Health Counselor
_____ Psychiatrist   _____ Marriage and Family Therapist
_____ School Psychologist   _____ Not in Mental Health Field
_____ Clinical Social Worker   _____ Other:_____

Name of person completing this form:_____

◆   ◆   ◆

Professional Resource Press
P.O. Box 15560
Sarasota, FL 34277-1560

Telephone #800-443-3364

E-mail at mail@prpress.com

CTPD/11/98

Add A Colleague To Our Mailing List . . .

If you would like us to send our latest catalog to one of your colleagues, please return this form.

Name:_____
                          (Please Print)

Address:_____

Address:_____

City/State/Zip:_____
                     This is ☐ home ☐ office

Telephone:(_____)_____

This person is a:

_____ Psychologist   _____ Mental Health Counselor
_____ Psychiatrist   _____ Marriage and Family Therapist
_____ School Psychologist   _____ Not in Mental Health Field
_____ Clinical Social Worker   _____ Other:_____

Name of person completing this form:_____

◆   ◆   ◆

Professional Resource Press
P.O. Box 15560
Sarasota, FL 34277-1560

Telephone #800-443-3364

E-mail at mail@prpress.com

If You Found This Book Useful . . .

You might want to know more about our other titles.

If you would like to receive our latest catalog, please return this form:

Name:_____
(Please Print)

Address:_____

Address:_____

City/State/Zip:_____
This is ❐ home ❐ office

Telephone:(_____)_____

I am a:

_____ Psychologist		_____ Mental Health Counselor	
_____ Psychiatrist		_____ Marriage and Family Therapist	
_____ School Psychologist		_____ Not in Mental Health Field	
_____ Clinical Social Worker		_____ Other:_____	

◆   ◆   ◆

Professional Resource Press
P.O. Box 15560
Sarasota, FL 34277-1560

Telephone #800-443-3364

E-mail at mail@prpress.com

CTPD/11/98